Life and Food in
the Basque Country

Life and Food in
the Basque Country

María José Sevilla

NEW AMSTERDAM
Lanham • New York • Oxford

NEW AMSTERDAM BOOKS
4720 Boston Way
Lanham, MD 20706

First published in the United States in 1990 by
New Amsterdam Books
by arrangement with Weidenfeld & Nicolson, Ltd., London.

All illustrations by Clifford Harper.
Translated from Spanish by Juliet Greenall.

ISBN 1-56131-035-2   (pbk. : alk. paper)

Printed in the United States of America.

CONTENTS

ACKNOWLEDGEMENTS

The *Life and Food of the Basque Country* began at the Oxford Food Symposium in 1987 when I was talking to Vicky Hayward about a theme which for years has occupied the majority of my free and professional time: the people of my country, their food and drink and in particular their gastronomic culture. Without Vicky's encouragement and enthusiasm this book would probably never have been written.

While the Basques' character and respect for tradition has always attracted me, their generosity has proved to be overwhelming. My gratitude to Pedro, Kika, Patxi, Asensio, Milagros, Antonio, Joseba, the Lasa family, Domingo, Nunchi, and to all who have so actively contributed to the reality of the chapters which follow. The linguistic ability of Juliet Greenall and Suzannah Gough and the patience of Philip, Daniel and Angeles have proved invaluable.

The Basque Country

INTRODUCTION

Who are the Basques: where do they live; what language do they speak? Where does their passion for action and freedom, their staunch individuality and, above all, their love of good food come from? What today is known as the Basque Country, or 'Euskadi', consists of the provinces of Baja Navarra, Labourdie and Zuberoa on French soil and Alava, Guipúzcoa, Vizcaya and Navarra in Spain.

The Basques have always been seen by the other inhabitants of the Iberian Peninsula as rather brusque, with great sincerity and strength of character, with an unswerving attachment to tradition, deeply religious, and with an obvious seafaring vocation. The novelist, Pio Baroja, wrote: 'I cannot define the Basque character concisely; all that I can say is that most of them have a warlike streak, that nearly all those who inhabit the countryside are slow of understanding, and that they are men of few words, who are rarely idle; calm, thoughtful and silent.'

The land where they have lived since prehistoric times lies either side of the western end of the Pyrenees, both inland and along the coast washed by the waters of the Cantabrian Sea. As you travel from Castile into the Basque Country villages, clustered around churches as though in search of shade, begin to stretch out along a single street, until eventually they become completely isolated farmsteads. The contrasting landscapes are sometimes calm and tranquil: the wheatfields of Alava, the maize plantations of Guipúzcoa, picturesque little fishing villages; at other times they are harsh and moody with a series of cliffs or mountain-peaks, partially clothed in luxuriant, leafy beechwoods, and with barren crags showing the harsh limestone rock at its most beautiful and unyielding; it changes mood dramatically according to the capricious and unpredictable climate. Hours of calm and blue skies may suddenly give way to unexpected and noisy storms when thunder and lightning rage furiously, the wind roars and the sound of the leaves as they rustle against each other is like an angry sea.

According to Father Barandiarán, one of the great experts on Basque matters, this is a culture which goes back 50,000 years. For his part, the ethnologist, Julio Caro Baroja, feels that one cannot speak of the 'Basque Race' since, apparently, up to the present-day all attempts to clarify the origins of such a race have proved useless and are lacking in scientific rigour. On the other hand, Baroja maintains that it is possible to speak of a 'Basque Tongue' – in his view an obvious survival of languages which predate the Indo-European invasion and, according to him 'whose form may have changed, but which survives'. The same author believes that the Basque language is related to that of the Aquitaine of south-west France.

In fact there are four main Basque dialects and more than twenty dialectic variations and subdialects. According to the historian, Martín de Ugalde, the Basque tongue and the Basque race are two mysteries which refuse to be solved or to die out in this corner of the Pyrenees.

Unamuno, the great philosopher and Basque writer, wrote of his nation: 'Until recent times it has played only a minor role in the live drama of History'. It has been said that since nations without a history are said to be fortunate, the Basques must certainly have considered themselves so for century after century, as they danced and sang in their mountains. The Nation has apparently looked on as others have undergone centuries of change and thus has succeeded in protecting its special character and, more importantly, its language. The Basques have not related or written down their own history, with the result that this has always been subject to interpretation by others.

From what we do know of the history of the Basques, we are conscious of a warlike, independent spirit, which is indivisibly linked with the sea. Navigators, adventurers and fishermen, the Basques have sailed the oceans and seas in search of lands, gold, adventure and fish. It is very probable that during the Roman occupation in the second century Basque vessels were used to transport minerals and it has been established that during the Norman invasion around AD 858 the Basques defied the invaders from the North and built ships in order to defend themselves by sea.

Focusing on Basque cuisine, or the several Basque cuisines, we can say that, above all, they are based on the sea and the mountains; one cannot isolate a country and its cooking from each other since one identifies the other. In this book I have tried not to write a complete cookery compendium; what I have attempted to do is to reflect the perfect duality that exists between man and food in the Basque Country, to the point where it becomes, to all intents and purposes, an obsession. People talk about cooking in just the same way as they might about the weather, or their children, that is to say, in most cases knowledgeably and to the point. Although it may mean that as a result they are unable to pay the February rent, nevertheless, on the day of the San Sebastián Tamborrada (drum parade), come what may, they will eat their *'casuelita' de angulas al pil-pil* ('little dish' of elvers cooked with chilli) and spend a good while telling their friends that the best sort are the ones with the black backs. It is simply a question of understanding their order of priorities and, as far as the Basques are concerned, the delights of the table head the list. In the words of Julio Caro Baroja: 'Basques are not interested merely in quantity, they always look for quality'. I shall always remember the harsh words of a Basque cook on the *piperade* prepared in front of the television cameras by a well-known British cookery presenter; what had offended her most of all was not the man's ignorance of the correct ingredients for the dish, but the levity with which they had been prepared. As far as she was concerned Basque cooking was something to be taken seriously, with no place for frivolity.

If I close my eyes and conjure up a scene of Basque cooking it takes the shape of an earthenware dish, cooking either on a farmhouse range, or on a stove in a Gastronomic Society kitchen; the first tended by a woman, the second by a man. In both cases we are talking of a style of cooking which is basically home and family cooking and which has always been passed on by the old women to the young ones who will eventually come to take their place. We are talking about cooking in a society which men, incorrectly, describe as 'matriarchal' – certainly not true of the Basque Country, where it is not the women who wear the trousers; the fact of the matter is that in this society the areas of responsibility are, or at least have been until now, very clearly delineated, particularly with regard to life in rural areas and little fishing towns, and until relatively recently this was the only sort of life that existed in such places. There can be no doubt that in the Basque Country it is the women who are the driving force behind all sorts of activities, but it is a far cry from being a society where the women give the orders. Nevertheless, we are talking about cooking which is also done by men, although outside the home, in Gastronomic or Sporting Clubs, at sea, in the open-air and in the competitions which they are so fond of. Everybody without exception considers patience in preparing and cooking the dishes properly to be absolutely essential. In practice it is traditional cooking which is the most important, in spite of the new trends which are felt even here, thanks to the defenders and promoters of the new Basque cuisine, which, to give it its due, has achieved well-deserved prestige.

Talking about Basque cooking, the chef Pedro Subijana says: 'It would be very difficult to define this cuisine precisely. It has its roots in the cooking of the people and it is true to its culinary traditions and practice. There are slight variations between the cooking of the different provinces of Guipúzcoa, Vizcaya, Alava and Navarra, but they all pride themselves on using local produce in season. Basque cuisine has several different sources of inspiration, ranging from peasant dishes to the cuisine of the bourgeoisie; it is alive and constantly evolving, without losing its uniqueness and identity; it is very close to the heart of all Basques'.

Although the portraits in this book depict the men and women of the southern Basque Country, I should like to add a few words on French-Basque cooking, which is undeniably an inseparable part of the whole. Its main characteristic is that it is an inland cuisine, relying on the fruits of the soil, with a bias towards dishes using meat, together with maize, the cereal which came to revolutionize the life of the Nation when it arrived from the Americas; these are the twin pillars on which depends its success. This is an obvious contrast to Spanish-Basque cuisine, which, although it also incorporates inland dishes, is at its most characteristic when it creates delicious dishes using the fruits of the sea. *Piperade, poulet basquaise* and *gâteau basque* may be seen as the acme of French-Basque cooking, which also relies on high quality ingredients such as Bayonne ham. Many of us have enjoyed a tasty *Cassoulet* at some time, or a good plateful of *Eltzekaria*, an ancient soup whose name derives from the word '*Eltze*', or 'cooking pot' in the Basque language, or that grand fish soup '*Ttoro*'. And I wonder what sweet could possibly compare with a preserve of cherries from the garden served with a selection of '*fromages de brebis*'?

MARKET DAY AT ORDICIA

Every Wednesday morning at first light, a fleet of vans and cars loaded with fresh fruit and vegetables, cheeses, loaves of bread, cakes, clothes and hardware, converge on the town of Ordicia on the banks of the river Oria. As the sun begins to rise behind the small town, huddled in the mountains, the market swings swiftly into action. The streets of the old quarter running away from the main town square and market place, become suddenly busy and stall holders put up stripy canvas awnings to protect their wares from the rain, which often falls at the most inopportune moment. Some of the country people simply sit down on a stool and arrange their goods around them in three or four baskets on top of a couple of wooden boxes.

In the echoing stone market building itself, foodstuffs, fresh fruit, vegetables and flowers are being unloaded by traders, farmers and householders who have come in to town to sell their produce. They take enormous care displaying their goods, arranging fruit and vegetables, according to variety, in large locally made wicker baskets arranged on folding trestle tables and displaying smaller items like honey, dried fruit, cheese and butter on spotless red-and-white checked tablecloths. Many of the stalls are separated by tall shelf-units, where some of the best goods, like prize cheeses, are on show, and fronted by glass display-counters where cut cheeses are stacked one on top of the other.

As the stalls fill up and conversations are shouted across the aisles, the noise echoes around the high ceiling and columns. This honey coloured stone building, with its vague pretensions to classical grandeur, reflects the historic importance of the market at Ordicia as one of the most traditional in the country; a free market whose prices have for centuries set a guideline and provided a reference throughout the rest of the province. The first charter authorizing the holding of the market was conceded by King Alfonso the Wise on 30 June 1268, but it was Doña Juana la Loca, Joan the Mad, daughter of the monarchs Ferdinand and Isabella, who re-endorsed the charter in 1512 in order to make restitution to the town for the terrible losses suffered from a fire, and laid down that the market should be held every week on Wednesdays. 'It is my wish and will', said Doña Juana 'that they should be able to sell, change and exchange in the said town and within its walls, from daybreak on the said market-day, until sunset, all and whatsoever chattels and goods of whichever sort.' Curiously, the market was not held for nearly three centuries – the reason being is not known for certain although there are various theories such as the lack of foodstuffs to sell – but since 1798 it has taken place every week without fail. Inevitably in recent years it has lost much of its original relevance, though its fame and quality still reflect the Basque passion for good food.

Outside the market-hall it is a beautiful morning. As the town begins to wake up, the square and streets around it are filled with possibilities and hope. The spring sunshine intensifies the brightness of the mosaic of objects, foodstuffs and people. On one side of the square the townhall clock, with its original black numerals against a white face and the town's coat of arms – a castle and a crown – are reminders of a noble past. The other three sides are lined with imposing grey stone buildings with wrought iron balconies topped by gleaming metallic spheres. They recall the nineteenth-century industrial revolution which took place here long before the rest of Spain. Under their arches merchandise is bought and sold as the morning proceeds.

The women, some young and some white-haired, close their doors behind them – housework already done. A couple of middle-aged men wearing the *txapela*, the traditional black Basque beret, are standing in the middle of the street, smiling broadly and shaking hands on the sale of three of the best animals to be found in the area. There is an almost tangible fiesta mood, *alegría de la fiesta*, in the air.

As far as most men are concerned, a visit to one or other – or several – of the neighbouring taverns is essential before any buying or selling. In every bar along polished wooden counters are ranged *tapas* to tempt the appetite of even the least hungry: plates of local black pudding, fried tongue, chunks of salt-cod coated in egg and flour and fried. The two beret-clad farmers move off to Conchita's cellar-bar, hidden on the corner of the square, to close their bargain over their first glass of wine of the day, a three-year old Rioja *tinto*. Usually everyday honest plonk or even rougher stuff is drunk in the bars, but market days are special and the extra cost is worth it. They decide to sample the black pudding and the cod as well and the waiter arranges small pieces on a plate, anchoring them with a toothpick to a slice of bread baked at dawn. The conversation begins as usual with the weather and then moves on to the outlook of the day's market, with complaints about the scandalous prices of *zizak* (wild mushrooms). Around the bar, the voices rise and fall, inevitably discussing the declining quality of life: the dancing at fiestas has changed; since the men gave up wearing dancing slippers things are not as good as they used to be. Their next stop will be in a couple of hours time when one of the friends insists on doing the honours as he seals yet another deal.

As opening time for the shops approaches, the bars empty and the crowd in the narrow streets which lead into the market square thicken. Soon it is difficult to make one's way through the town centre. There are foodstuffs, clothes, livestock, every sort of portable good; grocers, confectioners and butchers are all doing a roaring trade, too. In the cake shops, almond and pinenut tartlets and hundreds of glass jars containing multicoloured sweets, draw the children to the windows and they pester their mothers to spend some money. Silenced by the glass of the shop windows, the sales assistants are engaged in dressing them. The butcher, proprietor of a very modern shop, is pointing out his selection of dozens of *txistorras*, spicy sausages draped from a metal bar, to the crowds outside – their deep orange colour almost surpasses the garments displayed in a neighbouring frock shop window. In the same window there are shiny black local sausages, legs of lamb, tripe, best quality chops, all meat from animals which have grazed on the best pasture and which the butcher has had transported to the local abbatoir for slaughter.

Every so often one comes across a stall selling goods associated with the life of the surrounding valleys and the mountains. There are *albarcas*, the rubber galoshes used by the country people to protect their feet from the mud and puddles, cow bells, made of shining and sonorous metal, rough bladed knives and even a little stall specializing in military caps. In some of these streets creatures such as hens, sheep and cattle are also for sale, but this is a more specialized trade whose survival is nearing an end.

Here and there are local farmers' wives with jars of home-produced honey neatly labelled according to the sort of flower the bee has enjoyed, and covered with checked material to match the neatly hemmed tablecloth. Beside the honey there are often flat baskets of biscuits, the delicate *tejas*, literally, curved tiles, which are a local delicacy of nearby Tolosa. There are two types, plain ones and more expensive ones filled with almond morsels.

To make **Tejas** you need 6 whisked egg whites, 200g (7oz) of ground almonds, 100g (3½ oz) of flour and 200g (7oz) of caster sugar. Some confectioners recommend using 2 whole eggs with 4 whites, as the result has more flavour. In a bowl, mix well all the ingredients and place spoonfuls (quite small ones) on a greased baking tray. Put into a moderate oven (150°C, 300°F, Gas mark 2) until cooked. The easiest way of shaping them is around a rolling-pin as they come out of the oven and before they cool.

Grouped together in one section are the bakers' stalls with baskets holding different types of bread, some made from wheat flour, others from maize, and easily recognized by their orange tinge and the cabbage leaf underneath them, but both golden, crusty and rounded, with a slit cut in the centre, and lightly dusted with flour. Then there are long loaves weighing half a kilo of the sort which in Castile are known as *de pistola*. If ever factory-made sliced loaves succeed in replacing the different types of bread of the Basque Country, one of the great pleasures of good, simple fare will be lost for ever.

Nearby is the fresh produce from the farmsteads: flowers and root and green vegetables, which change according to the season. Here, too, the stallholders take great pride in the presentation of their bunches of dwarf spinach, its leaves an intense green on thin purple stems, tied together with green, red and yellow ribbons; two or three different varieties of cabbage, and small and large leeks; carrots and chard; asparagus, tender baby carrots, tiny potatoes, large potatoes, some red, some white; artichokes from Tudela with a label stating their origin, and with traces of reddish earth sticking to them as a result of the last few days' rain to prove that they have come straight from the rich soils close to the river Ebro. There are also baskets of seedlings ready for planting. The *casera*, or farmer's wife, often prefers to buy plants like this, which have made a good start.

Today new waves of cooking and healthy habits are being encouraged and are introducing a much wider range of vegetables to the daily Basque diet. In fact, the use of green vegetables in Basque cooking, at least as it is understood now, is relatively recent. A few decades ago root vegetables were preferred and few people made use, in their daily diet, of most of the varieties which now often form the first course in the housewife's menu.

Spring is the season of the *menestra*, a mixture of braised vegetables and originally a traditional Navarrese dish, but now made throughout the rest of the Basque country. The recipe, which comes from the town of Tudela in Navarre, can be considered one of the most authentic versions of the dish which has been adapted recently by *la nueva cocina* chefs to use baby spring vegetables.

 To make **Menestra** for two people, prepare 6 trimmed small artichokes, 250 g (8 oz) of fresh peas, 2 stems of silver beet or chard (or, if that is not possible, spinach will do), cut small, 150 g (5 oz) of green beans, a small tin of asparagus (*al natural*), 3 thin slices of *chorizo* sausage (preferably from Pamplona), a rasher of cured ham weighing 100 g (3½ oz), 1 tablespoon of flour, some olive oil, white wine, and the water from cooking the artichokes and a pinch of salt. Each vegetable must be boiled separately since they all have different cooking times. Start with the peas. Peel and cut the artichokes into quarters and cook them. Reserve the water from boiling the artichokes. Using another pan, cook the beans and then the silver beet. These are then dipped in egg and flour, as are the artichokes, and fried in olive oil until golden. Next, put a little olive oil in an earthenware dish and, once it is hot, add the ham and the *chorizo*, both cut into small squares; after a minute or two add a little wine and a glass of the artichoke water. Add the flour and stir well with a wooden spoon until the sauce thickens a little and the flour is cooked. Add a pinch of salt, taste and add the various vegetables, finishing with the asparagus and then bring back to the boil. There should not be much liquid left. Traditionally, in Navarre, *menestra* is accompanied by *rosé* or red wine.

Next to one of the stalls stands a tall, very dark man, bearded and thin faced, with a large basket of wild mushrooms. He leaves them with the stallholder, and a small crowd of buyers immediately gathers round. The Basque Country is, by any standards, a veritable fungus' paradise, and thanks both to its climate and habitat, mycology is a passion here. All sorts of lectures, cookery demonstrations and competitions, like a famous contest at Tolosa, are held to celebrate the richness of fungi. Every weekend keen amateurs scout the hillsides, woods and meadows, searching among the bracken and fine grasses. The large number of varieties which can make one unpleasantly ill, adds spice to the hunt; the Basque spirit is always drawn by elements of risk and danger. But every year the task of both professionals and amateurs becomes more difficult as the favourite local varieties become more scarce. Gradually the chestnuts and oaks which covered large expanses of terrain have given way to pine trees and with these have appeared new varieties of mushrooms, such as the *níscalos*, which now grows in abundance to the detriment of more valued varieties. Accordingly, the prices of the many varieties of fungi on sale in specialized shops and markets, bought by housewives, gastronomic society cooks and chefs, rise all the time but the Basque people are prepared to pay the price; elsewhere, it would be considered exorbitant.

Ordicia is known for its fungi stalls, although nobody ever knows what mushrooms will be on sale until the mushroom hunters arrive at the market. Today there is great excitement because the first spring-time *zizak* mushrooms, the most highly prized of all are available. The price label reads 12.000 pesetas a kilo, for the same price you could buy two pairs of excellent shoes, yet there are plenty of people ready to pay this sum of money.

These *zizaks*, belonging to the *Tricholoma* group which comprises three species, the *Tricholoma georgii*, *Tricholoma gambosum* and *Tricholoma albellum* are yellowish-white in colour with the cup rather deeper than the stem; they are small and have a delicious aroma. The people of Alava province consider them the best variety of all, they come into their own during the celebrations for the patron saint of the province, San Prudencio de Armentia, on 27 April, when they are eaten in huge quantities.

 The dish which has brought them renown is **Revuelto de zizak**, scrambled eggs with *zizak*; this recipe does justice to all their flavour and intense aroma. For each person you need 150 g (5 oz) of *zizak* mushrooms, 2 eggs, salt and a little olive oil. To prepare it wipe the mushrooms clean and break up the largest ones with your fingers, leaving the smaller ones whole (they may be tiny). Put a little olive oil to heat in a frying-pan, add the mushrooms and cook on a moderate heat. This type of mushroom gives off quite a lot of liquid which should be reduced as they cook, still on a moderate heat. Beat the eggs lightly in a bowl and pour into the frying-pan, stirring them into the mushrooms with a wooden spoon. Remove from the pan before the eggs set and serve immediately while the eggs are still soft.

The *zizak* at the market when I went there were collected by Francisco Gainza, a professional mushroom hunter, native of Ordicia, where he lives with his wife and family. A serious man, he rarely smiles, but when he does his face is cut open by a broad grin; he laughs infectiously. He has been gathering mushrooms since he was a boy and although this only provides him with a modest income, it allows him to do what he most enjoys in life, which is to walk and to be in contact with the natural world. Only between mid-winter until early spring, when mushrooms are scarce all over the country, does he sometimes take on some sort of temporary job in Ordicia.

Francisco divides his time between the mountains of Urbasa, La Sierra del Aralar and the area surrounding the town, according to the seasons and the varieties of fungi which appear in them. He knows exactly where to look and his years of experience tell him which sites to visit in search of signs. Sometimes it may be a particular species of tree, at others how the grass grows in a specific site or the weather conditions in a particular area during the last few days. He drives as close as he can to the site, then unloads his equipment: a pair of stout boots, thick woollen socks of the type used by the shepherds, a waterproof, a small wicker basket and a walking stick. From this point on, he walks, visiting the most likely sites. All the time he scans the undergrowth with his hawk-eyes, moving his head slowly from side to side. On some days he senses that his hunt will be successful because he can almost scent the mushrooms in the air. When he spots the black or grey species he has been searching for, he crouches down to examine them; then he pulls them up carefully, wipes them a little and puts them into his basket. After three hours he may only have found a few mushrooms, but they will be enough to make his trip worthwhile.

Francisco's skill is based on experience, distilled into instinct, and knowledge. He can identify the hundreds of varieties of mushroom and knows exactly which ones will appear first around Ordicia, then on the Aralar range and later in the Orduña area. He will never confirm or deny what he may have found or how many and he may even double back on his tracks if he thinks that a rival is following his trail. Anyone who goes with him is sworn to secrecy. He will tell his customers only that the *zizaks* have come from the hillside slopes and meadows around Ordicia.

Francisco searches out the different varieties with the changing seasons. He thinks one of the tastiest spring fungi is the *karraspina* (*Morchela esculenta*) which is usually served stuffed with small pieces of cured ham cooked on a griddle with a little oil and garlic sauce. This is a good method to prepare mushrooms lacking flavour. Delicious, too, is the *Coprinus comatus*, which is picked in the pastures and gardens during April. In summer there are at least half a dozen varieties: the various species of Russulas, best of all the *Guibelurdiñas* or *Russula cynaxanta*. This is enormously popular and cooked at its best by the *nueva cocina*, the new style of cookery, and the *Russula cirescens*, or *Idi min* in Basque, which is marinaded for salads with a little oil and cider vinegar; the adaptable *Ziza-ori* or *Saltxaperretxiku* in Basque (*Cantharellus cibarius*), is sometimes cut into slices and eaten raw in salads or simply used as a garnish for meat dishes or dried for enjoyment during the winter. In August the *Kuletos* (*Amanita caesarea*), a beautiful orange colour with a most delicate flavour, appears among the chestnut trees. Sadly it is now threatened by the disappearance of the chestnuts. It is best cooked in scrambled eggs, fried, barbecued or dressed with a little garlic, parsley and olive oil. Finally, there is the field mushroom, which has two different names in Basque. When it is still very young and its gills are reddish, it is known as the *Berrengorri*, but when mature it is called *Azpibeltz*, which describes its darker colour. It is delicious cut very finely and cooked in a moderate oven for twenty minutes with a little garlic, olive oil and parsley. On the whole it tends to be undervalued in Euskadi, the Basque name for their Country, where it grows of its own accord.

But autumn is the mushroom season *par excellence*. It is then that one can find the first examples of the fleshy *Clitocybe* group, which lend themselves to grilling and stewing. The black mushrooms (*Boletus Aereus*), found in resinous woodland and lightly forested beechwoods, are at their best sautéed with fresh herbs and a touch of garlic. New style Basque cookery makes a terrine with them. October is the month of the *Esnegorri* (*Lactarious delicious*), *Níscalo* in Castilian is probably amongst the best-known fungi in Spain, which has an orange tinged cap with spots underneath; it is found in pinegroves and is shipped in large quantities to Catalonia, where it is called *Rovellón*. Amongst the grass and the impressive yellows and ochres of the landscape, one finds the slender *Galanperna*; its cap resembling a Philippino sunshade. Sometimes it is cooked in batter, other times simply grilled. *Galanperna* is the Basque name of *Lepiota Procera*, or the 'Parasol' in Castilian. The *zizak* reappear now, as do dishes made with the simple, popular fungus, *Pholiota Aegerita*, or the thistle fungus, *Pheorotus aringii*.

The essential point to remember when cooking these mushrooms, as good Basque cooks will tell you, is to give each variety the appropriate cooking time and to choose a method according to their size, flesh, and if they are a very aromatic variety or need extra ingredients to improve their natural qualities and flavour.

 This is Francisco's recipe for cooking all sorts of **Mushrooms**, except *zizak*. You need about 500g (1lb) of mushrooms, 2 chopped cloves of garlic, 1 tablespoon of chopped parsley, 1 tablespoon of fine breadcrumbs, a little butter, olive oil and 50g (1¾ oz) of fatty bacon cut up small. In an earthenware dish Francisco browns 1 clove of garlic in the olive oil. He removes the dish from the heat and adds the whole mushrooms, the rest of the finely chopped garlic, the parsley and breadcrumbs. On top he puts the butter, a pinch of salt and the bacon. Then he puts this in the oven for about fifteen minutes, at 225°C (435°F, Gas mark 7). If the mushrooms are not so flavoursome like the famous *Guibelurdiñas* of the Russulas family, he adds a little wine and omits the bacon and breadcrumbs.

Francisco's best customers are the proprietors of restaurants in San Sebastián and Bilbao and even Madrid, but he also sells to one or two market stalls since they will buy the humbler varieties too and remain loyal customers.

Near the stall selling Francisco's mushrooms stands a sturdy woman with suntanned hands surrounded by two sacks of dried beans, one variety almost black in colour, the other of broad beans, and an interesting selection of smoked cheeses. She speaks with that suggestion of terseness and suspicion which characterizes the women of the north. 'Men are nothing but trouble', she remarks, 'specially mine'. Her name is Miren. She has been coming to the market since she was a child, when she kept her mother company on a stall in almost the same place as she now has her own. Once she was the cook of the famous Nicolasa restaurant in San Sebastián, but she had to leave her job when she got married. She is happy living in her *caserío*, or farmhouse, and would not change her life for anything, but coming to the market means a change, a rest, and she always goes home with good takings.

The beans that she brings down from the *caserío*, weighed out into kilos, are the staple diet of the Basque winter kitchen and grown throughout the Basque Country. They figure daily on the farmhouse table for the midday meal and often, too, in city homes and in all the restaurants, including the leading lights of the new Basque cuisine in San Sebastián, Madrid or Bilbao.

 Las Alubias de Tolosa are cooked in the following way. You need 1 kg (2 lbs) of black beans, 1 onion, 8 tablespoons of olive oil, 3 cloves of garlic, 2 small green chilli peppers (not hot), 250 g (9 oz) of pork ribs and salt. Put the beans in a large pot and cover with water. Add the chopped onion, green peppers and four dessertspoons of olive oil. Cook for about four hours at a low heat. One and a half hours before the cooking time is over, add the pork ribs, and fifteen minutes before, a *refrito* of garlic and olive oil prepared in a frying-pan. Season with salt. Often the *alubias* are served accompanied by cabbage, black pudding and *chorizo* previously cooked.

Before the fifteenth century and the arrival of different members of the bean family, only broad beans were known. They were dried to become *baba-txikik* and formed one of the most important parts of the diet of the Basques who worked every day in the fields. But after the discovery of the New World they were largely ousted by different varieties of the haricot bean, which soon became a popular part of the daily diet, unlike potatoes, which, curiously were considered fit only for animal fodder. From the sixteenth century the ubiquitous *potaje* or soup, which traditionally was made from chickpeas in Andalucía, Castile and Extremadura, became *Olla de Alubias*, literally pot of beans, to be eaten and enjoyed over the centuries. In Navarre some of the first of the crop are usually used to make various dishes using fresh haricot beans known as *pochas*. These are the fully grown mature beans, before they have dried out. Eaten fresh, the beans have a crunchy texture and consistency which gives a unique character to the dishes prepared with them. Abu Zacaria, a twelfth-century inhabitant of Seville, commented, referring to the culinary value of all legumes – 'they should be harvested early, before they are completely dried, not only are they easier to cook, but are much more enjoyable, with a more delicate flavour'. One dish above all, *Pochas con codornices* (Quail with pochas), is considered to be a Basque triumph.

 To make **Pochas con codornices** you need 500 g (1 lb) of *pochas* in their pods, a glass of dry white wine, 6 plucked and drawn quails, 2 carrots, a little lard, a little olive oil, 2 finely chopped cloves of garlic, 3 skinned and chopped tomatoes, 1 green pepper and some water. Sometimes a dried red pepper is added, but it is not traditional in my family. Put the beans – podded just before, so that they are still fresh – in an earthenware casserole and cover with cold water. Place on a moderate heat so that they cook slowly; do not stir them with a spoon but rock the dish gently from side to side so that they do not break. In a frying-pan fry the tomatoes and once they are done, add the chopped green pepper and cook until soft. Remove from the heat and purée. Add the sauce to the beans just before they finish cooking. Adjust the seasoning. In another earthenware dish put the quails with the wine, lard and a little olive oil, the peeled and chopped carrot and a little water. Cook for half an hour and then add the quail to the dish of beans, together with a little of the juice from cooking them. Bring to the boil once more and serve the quail, using the beans to garnish them.

José Castillo, the famous chef, includes a different recipe for beans with quail in one of his best-known publications, *Recetas de Cocina de Abuelas Vascas (Recipes from the Kitchens of Basque Grandmothers)*. In this case the beans, which he says should be from the town of Puente La Reina in Navarre, are boiled with a little water, ham, chopped onion, raw tomato, red pepper and virgin olive oil. The quails are cooked separately again, but after having been dredged with flour. The dish is finished by mixing together the contents of the two casseroles.

The dried broad beans are cooked in the same way as haricot beans, but they always have to be soaked overnight. Before cooking the water must be poured off and fresh water added, then a little bit of bacon and a good few drops of olive oil are added. When my mother served these beans, or lentils, she would fry a little garlic and paprika in oil and put this on top of the stew before serving. Nowadays they are much less widely grown and really only broadly used in the Alava and Navarre areas.

Some of the goods on sale at the market are from specialized shops in San Sebastián, Tolosa and Guernica, who sell their merchandise here and at the same time buy hand-made products which are difficult to find elsewhere. Around the trade of the market small specialist shops have grown up too, like La Casa del Bacalao, the house of cod, hidden away down a side street. Here in an enormous, well-lit glass refrigerator, you can find two dozen different cuts of salt-cod; necks, snouts, flanks, cheeks, gill-pieces, jaws, medallions or heads, flakes for making omelettes, crumbs for fishballs. Some cuts of the fish – those with most gelatine and least bones, such as the snout – almost always are used for *Bacalao a la vizcaina*, one of the supreme Basque salt-cod dishes and the *penca*, part of the fish's main body, used for *bacalao al pil-pil* are very expensive. So also are the *kokotxas* or cheeks, a delicacy which is prepared in parsley, olive oil and garlic sauce. Near the counter stands a guillotine consisting of a blade whose tip is attached to a block of wood of the same length, which makes it very easy to cut the cod, and on a nearby counter a range of dishes are on show, demonstrating the correct cut of cod for a particular recipe, together with all the other necessary ingredients.

At first it may seem curious that salt-cod is still an important ingredient in Basque cookery since it is not an indigenous product of either the wild Cantabrian seas or the Mediterranean. Nor by any means, is it unique to the Basque Country: salt-cod has been eaten everywhere from Catalonia to Valencia, and Castile to Andalucía and is always easy to find in grocery shops and market stalls. In the *Mercado de la Cebada* or Barley Market, in Madrid, it is quite common to see customers leaning on the counter in the little cafés dotted around the area of the market hall, early in the morning, enjoying some fried *bacalao*, dried salt-cod, with a bottle of beer.

But there is a good historical reason for salt-cod remaining a popular food in the Iberian Peninsula and specially the Basque Country long after it had become an unusual ingredient elsewhere in Europe. One, of course, is the Roman Catholic religion with its long Lents and fast days. While, in the rest of Europe, the tradition of going without meat on Fridays and during Lent, had almost disappeared by the seventeenth century, in Spain it persisted. When I was a child my mother would religiously buy the obligatory parochial dispensation or *bula* – a Papal document granting concessions, immunities and indulgences, without which we could not eat meat on Friday every week of the year. Alongside this, other fish, such as hake also owe their popularity to the distinction of recipes for using it. Cooked with honey, spinach and pine kernels, used in salads or stews, combined with tomato or dried red peppers, cod is no longer regarded as a food of the poor, but a gastronomic delicacy, increasingly a treat for the minority who can afford it.

The Basques' particular fame for salt-cod dishes can also be ascribed to their long history as adventurous fishermen through vocation and necessity. They have always gone much further afield than other fleets (originally in pursuit of the prized whale), crossing the oceans as far back as the eleventh century and then by the sixteenth century fishing for cod in the cold waters of northern Europe and Canada, following the route of the Portuguese navigator Gaspar de Conte Real, who had discovered Newfoundland's shoals of cod, around 1560. For the next four centuries, the Basque fleet was catching enough fish to supply the country. It is only in the last few years that the fleet has almost entirely disappeared and practically all the cod is now imported from such places as Scandinavia and the Faeroe Isles.

When you discover the imagination and dedication that the Basques, and especially the *vizcainos*, the people of Vizcaya, have devoted to the culinary use of this disarmingly plain looking fish, you understand that the two are synonymous. There are, perhaps, a dozen classic dishes such as *Bacalao a la marinera* with potatoes and parsley, *Bacalao frito*, fried cod coated with egg, *Bacalao a la vizcaina*, with a rich sauce of *choricero* peppers and ham; but among these, one in particular, *Bacalao al pil-pil*, cod in a perfect emulsion of garlic, olive oil and the gelatine from the skin of the fish, stands out. According to the Spanish writer, José Carlos Capel, there is an amusing story attached to the way it was invented. He explains how shortly before the Second Carlist War, in the 1860s, a shopkeeper in Bilbao who specialized in salted goods ordered thirty or forty packs of dried cod from Norway but when the cargo was unloaded, discovered to his horror that his assistant had mistakenly copied out the order for 3,040 packs. Convinced that he was a ruined man, he had no choice but to take delivery of the mountain of cod. Shortly afterwards, the Carlist siege began and the shortage of food-stuffs of all kinds made our friend a rich man almost overnight. In culinary terms, the significant fact was that a chef had to hand only olive oil, some garlic and a few slices of dried salt-cod, and thrown back on his ingenuity, created the recipe and the technique of *'pilpileo'*, a wonderful onomatopoeic name for the noise made by the bubbling oil in the cooking process. Later on, another chef, by gently moving the *cazuela*, or earthenware pot, obtained the emulsified *Bacalao ligado*.

 To prepare **Bacalao ligado** for four people, we need 4 thin cod slices, 6 cloves of garlic, olive oil, 1 small chopped dried chilli pepper. Soak the fish for twenty-four hours. Change the water every eight hours and dry the fish. Lightly crush the garlic in a pestle-and-mortar, but do not make a paste. Cover the base of a medium-sized earthenware dish with olive oil, adding the garlic and placing the fish on top, the skin underneath. Pour over a little more olive oil until the fish is almost covered, add the chilli pepper, which is optional. From that moment until the end of the cooking move the dish gently back and forth over a moderate heat. Some small white bubbles will start appearing on top which eventually will help to thicken and bleach the sauce. Carry on cooking and tilting the dish until the oil has become a thick sauce with a lovely white colour.

The secret of all salt-cod dishes lies in the precise art of removing the salt from the fish. There are two possible methods used, depending on the recipe. The first is for the most elaborate Basque cod dishes and requires time and an expert eye, without which the result will be disappointing. The cod must be soaked in cold water for between twenty-four and thirty-six hours. The water must be changed two or three times. If the cod is slightly flaked before soaking then it will need less time. Too short a soaking time and the cod will be salty; too long, and it will lose all its magic taste and texture. The art of extracting the salt cannot be learnt in a mere day or two. I have to confess to more than one cod disaster, but one day you get it right, the recipe turns out perfectly and there is no looking back. The second, or rapid method, is mainly used for dishes such as *Ajoarriero* (potato, *bacalao*, garlic and red pepper dish) or *Zurrukutuna* (a substantial cod soup) in which the cooked cod is flaked and its finished texture not so important. First, the pieces of fish are grilled over hot coals or a hotplate for about three minutes to soften them and so making it easy to remove the skin and bones. Next, the cod is soaked in water for two or three hours. This method is a useful standby and means

Ajoarriero can be prepared within a morning. It is a delicious dish to which other ingredients such as tomatoes, chilli pepper or even lobster can be added. In Navarre, where it originated, nearly everybody has their own version.

 This particular recipe for **Ajoarriero** comes from my mother. For two people she uses 250 g (8 oz) of dried salt-cod, 3 cloves of garlic, ⅓ dried chilli peppers, 4 dried red peppers, 200 g (7 oz) of bread broken into small pieces, a little tomato sauce and a 250 ml (9 fl oz) of water, half of which is the soaking water from desalting the fish. Soak the *bacalao* for about twenty-four hours, or less if it is very thin, or use the rapid method, described above, if you are short of time. Change the water twice. Soak the dried red peppers for a few hours. When soft, remove the seeds and scrape the pulp from the skin with a teaspoon. Brown the garlic in an earthenware dish, add the pieces of bread, brown slightly, add the water and cook for a while. Add 2 generous tablespoons of tomato sauce, the pulp of a red, dried pepper, or *choricero*, and the chilli. Finally, add the dried cod, flaked. Cook very slowly for about one hour. It should have the consistency of a thick soup.

In spring and autumn, the arcades of the market place are crowded with small stalls selling fine, farmhouse sheep's milk cheeses. These are hand-made on the *caseríos*, or farmsteads, and in the shepherds' huts in the mountains of southern Guipúzcoa, Alava and Navarra, and are usually brought down to the market by the farmers' or shepherds' wives and daughters. These days, as the pastoral way of life begins to disappear, so too do the hand-made Basque cheeses; Roncal cheese, from the valley of the same name in the Pyrenees, is slightly pungent, with a distinct smokey flavour and a noticeable piquance which makes it popular as an end to a meal. The well-known cheeses of Idiazabal from the macizo de Aitzgorri in Guipúzcoa and the ones from the Aralar mountain range, which are similar, are yellow in colour, some lighter, some darker. The shepherds often smoke them using freshly felled wood, which gives them an orange-tinged rind and a characteristic flavour. They are cylindrical in shape, weighing between a kilo and a kilo and a half and when they are at their best, the cheese is easy to cut and has a few holes in it. If it is kept too long, it loses its pleasant fresh flavour and becomes rather salty and too brittle. Also famous are the Baztan cheeses, used as an apéritif or added to soups and *talos*, a maize cake, and the ones produced from Gorbea or Orduña. These days, each shepherd has his own enthusiastic customers who regularly place orders in the hope that there will be enough cheese to go round.

José Martín, a shepherd on the Sierra del Aralar, sells most of his cheeses at Ordicia through his daughter, María José, who drives over to the market every week. His father, who was also a shepherd, took him up to the mountains when he was eight. Those were hard times when everyone had to work to earn a meagre living. The first night that he spent alone in the *txabola*, a small hut built by his father of rubble, lime, moss and clay, he was so cold and frightened that he could not sleep a minute all night. The facilities of the hut consisted of a camp bed, an open hearth and a small space for making and storing the cheeses. Now, fifty years later, José Martín has just moved into a little cottage in the place of the original hut where he spent half of his life. Like the sheepfold which is just behind it, it is in a sheltered position, on a slight slope and protected by rocks. Nearby stand other huts, grouped together to form a settlement, or *saroiak*, which share small sheds or extensions. They also share sheepfolds of stone or woven hurdles linked by crosspieces; *gaztategui*, or dairy, where the cheese is made; *txerriteguo* or pigsty and *baratza* or kitchen garden, where they grow lettuce, potatoes, leeks, garlic, onions and fresh herbs such as parsley. The hens scratch about peacefully within the settlement. In the *egurtoki*, or woodstore, the logs wait ready to provide warmth or contribute towards cooking a good stew. Small herds of Pyrenean cattle and horses often live wild around the shepherds' settlements.

With the arrival of spring the shepherd leaves the valley and the plain and leads his flocks up to the cool, green summer pastures, which are generally common ground and subject to various regulations governing their use and tenure. They may belong to a single village, or several, or a whole valley. The shepherd will stay up there until, once more, the cold snow forces him to take refuge in the land below.

In summertime the life of the shepherds is simple and often lonely. Nowadays most of them are bachelors; in earlier times they used to get married, but now women are not willing to share their lives with a man who they see so rarely. Nonetheless, they reply unanimously that they prefer the life of a shepherd in the mountains. José Martín could never give up the months that he spent in the mountains with his sheep and his dogs. When he got married, he sold his sheep and, for a while, spent his time tending cattle to spend the summers with his wife, but it was not the life for him and gradually he got his flock together again and went back up to his beloved mountains. The love which this man feels for the shepherd's way of life and the mountains where he grew up is deep and intense. He derives his main satisfaction in life from walking with the dogs. Since he prefers to be alone with his thoughts, he has never owned a radio.

José Martín knows each of his sheep by name and, incredible as it may seem, they recognize him. They are Latxas, with long coats which look as though they have been parted along the sheep's back and combed, a breed which has evolved here since sheep were first domesticated in Neolithic times. Hardy animals, who prefer cold mountain pastures and sleeping out in the open air in summertime, they can be sold as lambs for meat and their fleece used for carpet making. The ewes give about a litre and a half of milk a day and are usually milked twice daily over 120 days.

Between the months of May and November, José Martín is alone with his sheep, he rises at six or seven o'clock each morning and, after a light breakfast of goat's milk and a little bread, goes out to milk his flock. Sometimes they have slept in the fold, at other times he has to go and find them and pen them in before milking. The warm milk squirts loudly into the plastic bucket as the shepherd squeezes the ewes' teats.

As soon as he gets back from milking José Martín sets about making the cheese. The first part of the process is to filter the still tepid milk. If the milk has cooled down too much he warms it gently to about 25°C. In the mountains the shepherds still use natural rennet, which they thin with a little warm water and add to the milk as it is filtered. The mixture is left to stand for three-quarters of an hour and then stirred with the hand or a spoon until the whey begins to separate from the curds. The liquid is drained off little by little and the curds pushed down to the bottom of a plastic bowl. At this point the curds are cut into the number of cheeses which he wishes to make. Each piece is placed in a plastic mould, left for a while and then turned over. Until a few years ago José Martín did everything by hand because he had no cheese press; now he has a small one where the cheese remains for about twelve hours, after which it is passed through a *salmuera* or brine solution, and then left for another twelve hours. Some shepherds simply cover the surface of the cheese with salt. Once they have been salted the cheeses are placed on some boards of wood where they are left for about two months, before being sold.

During the winter, in the *caserío* in the lowlands where José Martín lives with his family, they only make cheese once a day. 'After doing the evening milking we put the milk in the fridge. The following day we add the new milk to that of the previous night and heat it to 30°C'. Nevertheless José Martín says that the cheese made in the mountains is the best because the grazing is superior there, and, as a result, the milk is of a higher quality.

José has never found it hard to stand loneliness, but he could not tolerate being ill-fed. He learnt how to cook when he was doing his military service and always cooks carefully for himself in the mountains. Lunch is invariably a hot-pot known in Basque as *Eltzea*, a word also used to describe the slow-witted. Sometimes it is made from lentils, at others haricot beans or potatoes, but it always contains whatever green vegetables are available to the shepherd. The cooking pot is made of metal and lined in ceramic, not earthenware, and he puts it on one side of the hearth away from the direct heat so that his lunch cooks slowly while he takes the first rest of the day.

To make **Eltzea** for six people prepare 750g (1½ lbs) of good quality brown lentils, an onion, olive oil and a ham bone. Clean the lentils, removing the ones which looked a bit doubtful, and any small pieces of grit which have got into the bag, before putting them to soak overnight. Simply put into a stewing pot or casserole with ¾ of the onion, the ham bone and a good splash of best olive oil. Cover with water and put to cook on top of the stove until tender; it may be necessary to top up with more cold water. I like to add a bit of potato, cut into small pieces, about half an hour before removing the pan from the heat. Then prepare a *sofrito* – the remainder of the onion, finely chopped, and sautéed with a little paprika.

In the winter his wife Carmen does the cooking in the farmhouse. Two of her specialities are *Ollo salda*, or chicken broth and a walnut dessert, called *Intzaursalsa*.

 To prepare **Ollo Salda** you need 1 boiling-fowl, 2 average-sized leeks, 100g (3½ oz) of chick peas, 2 large carrots, a little parsley, cold water and several tablespoons of home-made tomato sauce. Put the boiling-fowl and the other ingredients in a large saucepan, cover with water and bring to the boil. As it boils scoop off the scum which forms on the surface and add several ladlefuls of fresh water, continuing this process until the broth is quite clear, and then leave it to simmer until the bird is tender. Remove the fowl from the pan, cut off the breast part and cut into small pieces; add these to the broth. Put the remaining pieces of the fowl, also jointed, into another saucepan, with the leeks and carrots on top, and a little of the tomato sauce which has been made previously. A few mushrooms can be sautéed in olive oil and also added. Serve the consommé as the first course, followed by the chicken pieces.

 Intzaursalsa is a very old recipe from the *caserío* where there are always one or two walnut trees which give an excellent crop each year. Prepare 200g (7oz) of shelled walnuts, 200g (7oz) of sugar, 1 cinnamon stick, ¾ litre (1¼ pints) of water and ¾ litre (1¼ pints) of milk. Traditionally the walnuts are crushed with a wooden mallet or coffee-grinder, having first been wrapped in a piece of thick, white cloth, until they formed quite a smooth paste. Then the water is boiled in a saucepan with the cinnamon and the walnut paste is added. This is left to simmer until the water has nearly evaporated, at which point the milk and sugar are added. The mixture is cooked until it thickens to form a light cream, which is served in individual dishes. A little ground cinnamon is sprinkled on to each dish before serving.

José Martín says that in his house, just as in his parents', there is no doubt that the woman wears the trousers, though he admits that both his mother, who was one of thirteen brothers and sisters, and his wife Carmen, have always recognized that there must be a spirit of equality. He also admits that Carmen is a very good cook and that is one of the reasons he married her. They met at the *Fiesta de San Martín* at the beginning of November, where traditional *jotas* were danced to accordion music every morning for several days. They danced in couples, but without touching and unusually, it was the woman who decided if she wished to change partners or not. The man had to go up to her and if she found him more attractive than the man she was dancing with, she would change partner. Apparently, the priest was always criticizing the women and girls, calling them to order when they seemed to be enjoying themselves more than was seemly, but after the dancing was over, everyone would go off to the tavern for a drink and sometimes the girls would go too, so that the men had the opportunity of seeing them home afterwards, which at that time was considered very forward. Soon after, on San Martin's day itself, José Martín decided that his bachelor days were over.

José Martín looks back to the old days with regret, life is so much easier today. The advent of the car has brought a great change to the life of the transhumant shepherd, making it very much easier to travel up and down the mountains. When he was young, José Martín would go down to the valley once a week to buy meat and fresh vegetables and to fetch water; nowadays his sons take all sorts of provisions up to him by car. Also, now that he has so much more space with the new house, his daughter, María José, and her family spend the weekends in the mountains with him. Yet at the same time he is still thinking about the past with great enjoyment. José Martín remembers the amazing spectacle of flocks of some hundred-thousand sheep in continual movement to and from the mountains and the lowlands. He knows that he will never see it again, he knows, too, that none of his children will become shepherds and that within fifty years his small cottage in the Aralar may become a weekend refuge for the family or worse still, may be a ruin. He also knows that the shepherds' cheese production will become a romantic idea for the people who knew about the unique taste of mountain culture.

THE CASERIO

As dawn breaks, Cándida Lasa goes downstairs to prepare break-fast. She makes nettle-tea for Millán, the eldest, white coffee for Pepita and black for José Luis. She and Lucas prefer some nice camomile tea. The men go to feed the livestock in the barn and do the milking, while the women see to the household tasks. The windows are open wide and the bed clothes are all hung out to air; by nightfall everything smells of spring.

A few hours later, the quiet of the house is broken as the brothers gather round the table again for *el almuerzo*, a light meal between breakfast and the midday meal. 'You have to feed them up,' says Cándida; 'a farmer's life is very hard.' Amongst the family she uses Basque language, which on her lips sounds soft and reminis-cent of Japanese. Some of the brothers are drinking cider, Millán and the women water; for the first few minutes they eat quietly enjoying the food and the fresh bread but soon they are all talking about the fields and the animals. On other mornings each brother has a plateful of fried eggs with ham which is home-cured when they kill the pig in November.

The farmhouse falls silent once more. From the kitchen window

Cándida can see her elder sister, Pepita, who is pulling the weeds which have appeared in the turnip patch after the recent rain. Pepita is a woman of great energy and character; she is small and slim, her dark complexion contrasting with that of the younger sister, who is fair and rosy. The two women have very different outlooks on life. Pepita is a rebel. There were two things which she wanted to be able to do when she was young. The first, to drive a car, she has achieved; the second, to swim, has remained beyond her reach. But she still dreams of diving into the crystalline waters of a river hidden in the mountains or into the Cantabrian sea.

Cándida's outlook is traditional. She has no desire to leave the farm where she was born and is content within the four walls of her home and the confines of the kitchen garden. The worst years of her life were those spent working in a factory in San Sebastián. In those days, when she was a girl, the farm did not produce enough income to support the whole family and since the province of Guipúzcoa was in the process of industrialization she found work in a factory. Others were not so lucky. Many of the local girls had to take jobs as maids anywhere they could, and the men had to leave the area for other places, even overseas. Cándida would have loved to live in the last century. Her mother only left the farm twice a year, to go to Murgia on San Prudencio's day and to Alsa on San Miguel's day. Some years she may have spent a couple of days away visiting her family, but that was all. Then, and for centuries before that, the *caserío*, or farmhouse, was the entirety of a woman's life. Even today Cándida goes no further than the village, where she sells milk and bunches of fresh vegetables that she cuts from the kitchen garden to sell to her regular customers. She goes every morning, setting off after the *almuerzo*. Today the sun is brilliant, its brightness accentuating the colours of the leaves, meadows and flowers. Cándida walks briskly; she is used to the weight of the milkcan and the wicker basket carrying the vegetables. She would not want to make the journey by car, even if she could drive. 'I wonder why we need all these cars invading the countryside,' she says, 'I used to love to see the carts drawn by oxen. I almost wish that there were no tractors, though

I can see they have helped the men a lot. But in the olden days we didn't have them and life went on just the same. When I think that one tractor costs as much as a beautiful yoke of oxen!' The grey and green hills and mountains spread before her as she walks. If an occasional ray of sunlight escapes from behind the northern clouds, then the beauty of the landscape is beyond words; everything looks fresh and new. One, two, three *caseríos*, a little church down in the valley. The *caseríos* are dotted here and there, every few kilometres, like droplets over the hillsides. Some are painted white; the grey stonework of others resists the prevailing harsh climate; the wind, rain and long, hard winters. These farmsteads, isolated, independent economic and social units, remain the heart of rural life, even since industrialization. In Basque symbolism they represent good, protecting all that is inside, whereas outside their walls lie danger and the unknown.

Throughout Euskadi, or the Basque Country, the roof tiles reflect the ownership of the property. Each *caserío* has a name. Sometimes it is called after the family who live or lived there, while with others the name has no apparent meaning, having developed over the centuries. Candida's and her brothers' and sister's *caserío*, for example, used to be known as Pagaduzuarza, then as Pagadizu, and eventually, by its present name, Pasus. Apparently the meaning is unknown. Pasus is situated in the mountain just a few kilometres from the village of Villabona in the province of Guipúzcoa. This *caserío* sits in a gentle hollow where several slopes meet and protect it from the winter winds. Nearby, there are always two or three small stacks of hay drying around poles to feed the animals during the winter. When the light falls, they look like large protective soldiers or characters from *Don Quixote*. Walnut trees, bearing green fruit in spring, line the road leading to the classical, somewhat austere house built some four hundred years ago; it is probably one of the oldest *caseríos* in the area. The pitched roof is of irregular hand made tiles and its two sides are slightly different in size. Part of the mortar is missing from the façade of the building and the stone shows through its worn, grey sides. Yet, it is very much a working farmhouse. To the left of the main doorway stands the cowshed. The front façade is unadorned with no painted brown, green, or red shutters, varnished beams or noble escutcheons and shields as reminders of past adventures or seas sailed. Instead there are six plain windows and the front door, shaded in summer by a beautiful mature vine. But the Basque farmhouse is not merely a building, it consists of the people and animals who live there, the fields which belong to it, the kitchen garden which feeds it. Furthermore, it represents a desire to achieve an almost impenetrable and self-sufficient unit.

Strictly speaking, Pasus might be considered an atypical farm. The parents of the Lasa brothers and sisters died many years ago and apart from one who married, the rest live together in the *caserío*. They are all unmarried and share their lives and inheritance. In this case there was no *mayorazgo*, the system whereby a chosen son inherits everything in exchange for staying to work the family farm. In no circumstances can it be divided up. There are also a nephew and niece who spend more time in Pasus than in their own houses. At Pasus it is the eldest sister and brother, Pepita and Millán, who make the decisions and Millán, the man who has the final word, except in purely domestic matters. It is the man who deals with the stock and machinery, sowing the crops and cutting the hay, caring for the cows and pigs. They also make the cider. The woman takes care of the kitchen and the house, the kitchen garden and the hens and hundreds of other household tasks.

All the land surrounding the house and much that is out of sight, belongs to Pasus; to the right is a large field planted with mangels and bordered by a row of apple trees. Some are the varieties thought best for cidermaking, others provide cooking apples. Next to the mangels is a field of turnips, with a patch of spare ground lying fallow, and another of potatoes. Opposite the house just beyond the road, is the kitchen garden, the women's domain. They plant and tend it, then prepare its fresh greens and root vegetables in the kitchen. However the farm's main income derives from meat and milk, most of which is sold to the dairy in the valley for a low but secure price. In addition, Cándida sells her few litres of milk every morning in the village.

There is a great difference between life in winter and in summer. In summer it is still light until half-past ten at night, whereas in winter they are ready to sit down to dinner at seven o'clock in the evening. 'We simply work until the light has gone', explains Millán. The brothers share out all the tasks. The cows are milked twice a day, morning and night. In the morning, after milking, they are driven out to graze. In summer the grass must be mowed nearly every day to provide fodder for the animals during the winter. In spring potatoes, maize and beans are planted, the latter amongst the maize plants so that they can climb up them.

Cándida and Pepita have divided up the traditional tasks of the *etxekoandre* or lady of the house, and organize their lives efficiently. Both sisters share the work in the vegetable and flower garden, Pepita organizes the house and Cándida, the younger, is official cook to the household and sees to everything that takes place in the kitchen, the most important part of the house, a simple and informal meeting place. A few years ago the brothers modernized it completely, putting in functional grey formica units and covering the walls with white tiles so that they are easy to keep clean without needing to be painted all the time. The canopy over the great fire-place has also been modernized, although today the fire is not lit and two reddish-coloured clay pots used for cooking chestnuts are the sole reminders of its warmth on winter evenings. However, all that is traditional has not yet disappeared. The floor is made of well polished terracotta tiles. The modern stove, with bottled gas, which was bought when the inside of the house was refurbished, is used for small speedy jobs, like cooking breakfast and the afternoon snack, but it does not yet compete with the cast-iron range. It is ancient in appearance, but was only acquired recently. The best part of the Pasus kitchen is the pantry. Almost as large as the kitchen itself, it is an orderly store-room. There are baskets of maize, sacks of reddish-black dried beans weighing more than twenty kilos, some small ones with lentils and chickpeas and another big one full of potatoes. Beneath the glass of the cheese dish, sit two fine sheep's milk cheeses. They used to make their own cheeses on the farm, but now they buy it from the shepherds who have huts nearby. Hanging from the ceiling are two hams and strings of a dozen cooking *chorizo* sausages and *txistorras*, traditionally made with pork, fat, garlic and salt, all marinated with paprika. Nearby are strings of garlic and dried *choricero* peppers, of two different sizes; *choricero* peppers are sweet. In a cupboard are a multitude of glass jars of different shapes and sizes, containing the preserves which are made every year at the farmhouse, some fruit and some vegetable, and a similar mixture of bags of flour and sugar and pots of spices and dried herbs such as oregano and bay leaf. High up on a shelf is a collection of locally made cider vinegar and wine vinegar which she uses for preserving and to make the salad dressing. There are also half a dozen bottles of cider, red wine and white *txakolí*, the dry and slightly *pétillant* wine of the Basque Country, just enough for the week. The rest is stored in Millán's cellar, where it keeps better. The only new addition to the kitchen is a large fridge-freezer that they bought a couple of years ago which has turned out to be one of their most useful new possessions. Inside are several chickens, a couple of ducks, a bit of bacon and some fish. Since there is a splendid fishmongers at Villabona Cándida has been able to get all kinds of fish instead of the *bacalao*, dried salt-cod, of the old days, although she still uses this every day. The freezer really comes into its own in winter, when the farm provides less variety, and shopping in the village means a cold, wet walk for Cándida.

By midday Cándida is in front of the range; this time cooking lunch, the main meal of the day. If it was up to her they would eat fish and vegetables day in day out; she is practically vegetarian and prefers simple dishes. 'How can anyone improve on some good fish cooked in a few drops of olive oil and a squeeze of lemon juice, or a salad of tomatoes and onions picked minutes before from the garden?' Pepita plants the tomatoes every April, under Cándida's kitchen window, a sheltered spot which gets plenty of sun. She plants two varieties, one early and one late, which keep the kitchen supplied well into the autumn. 'One year we still had tomatoes at Christmas', commented Pepita. She used to sow the seeds herself, but that is no longer necessary; nowadays she can buy the young plants at one of the local markets.

One of Cándida's recipes which makes good use of Pepita's tomatoes are **huevos al plato**, ham, tomato sauce, peas, *chorizo* and eggs cooked in a small cazuela, or earthenware dish. To prepare the eggs grease the dish with a little olive oil, add 2 tablespoons of tomato sauce and break open the eggs on top. Arrange in colour-order the rest of the ingredients and cook on top of the stove at a moderate temperature; this will allow the egg yolks to retain moisture while the whites are cooked.

The rest of the family do not agree with Cándida; their favourite dishes are different specialities of hers belonging to the Basque peasant-cooking of the interior, traditionally based on dishes made from meat and poultry, dry salt-cod and, sometimes, freshwater fish, and vegetables from the farm like leeks or cabbage. With these, she makes pasta, garlic or vegetable soups, cooks chicken and meat casseroles and excellent fish stews. Their taste is very traditional and new trends in cooking are of no interest to the family.

Lucas, one of the brothers, told me that their worst meals at home are on Sundays because his sister Cándida insists on making dishes which are foreign to the usual repertoire, such as a cold salad of potatoes, tinned tuna and peas in mayonnaise or rice cooked in a paella pan. 'Rice is for the Valencians and the Chinese', he says. For Cándida, their conservatism is a problem. 'My brothers always demand beans as their first course and that gets tiresome', explains Cándida. 'We eat beans every blessed day of the year.' The beans are traditionally planted amongst the maize so that it provides a support for the climbing plants. In this way, the brothers kill two birds with one stone and do not need to erect bean poles for them. Every day, Cándida cooks the beans with a little carrot and onion. The dish of chillies is empty and so Cándida tips in a few more from a jar. The family could not imagine eating red beans without some chillies to go with them. To prepare these she buys several kilos of the very small variety, then washes them and puts them in large glass jars with a chickpea and a clove of garlic. She fills each jar with half water and half wine vinegar; after a year in the larder, they will be delicious. The chillies at Pasus are yellow and very hot.

Pepita is laying clean plates and Cándida has put an enormous earthenware pot on the table. Today she has cooked *Lengua a la tolosana*, tongue in the style of Tolosa, a recipe highly thought of in the area around Pasus. Its only disadvantage is that the initial preparation is rather tedious; this involves cooking the calf's tongue in plenty of salted boiling water for about fifteen minutes, after which it is drained and skinned.

 To prepare **Lengua a la tolosana** for six people you need 1 good-sized calf's tongue, 1 glass of white wine, 1 glass of stock, 1 leek, 1 carrot, 1 large onion, 2 tomatoes, olive oil and salt. Put a little oil in a baking dish then add the tongue and the carrot, onion and leek all peeled and finely chopped, on top. Cook for about forty minutes at 200°C (400°F, Gas mark 6). Take it out of the oven and transfer to a deep earthenware dish, add the tomatoes, peeled and chopped, the wine and the tongue and pour over the stock and add a little water to cover. Bring to the boil, then reduce the heat and simmer gently until tender for about one and a half hours. Remove from the dish, slice and serve with the strained sauce poured over it.

Lucas likes all the food roasted and José Luis prefers all his in a sauce. 'How can I go along with that?' asks Cándida. But she does make an excellent *callos*, a tripe dish which will convert even the most sceptical.

 To cook **Callos** successfully the tripe must be of excellent quality and very clean. To feed four people you need 1 kg (2 lbs) good tripe. Wash it well in water to which a few drops of vinegar have been added. Rinse and then cut into small pieces. Put these into an earthenware casserole and boil until tender. Drain off the water. In another earthenware casserole fry 2 finely chopped medium-sized onions and 2 tablespoons of olive oil. Add the tripe and some home made tomato sauce and cover with meat or bone stock. Simmer gently for an hour and then a little chilli can be added for flavour. Sometimes Candida decorates the dish with red peppers.

But the family's traditionalism does not reflect a lack of interest in cooking; they truly enjoy the majority of the dishes and in particular Cándida's lunchtime puddings. The brothers are particularly fond of fruit compotes, whether summer or winter ones. The Pasus apples, particularly the Reineta variety, give them a very special flavour, slightly acidic but full of fruit. The secret of these compotes which consist of fruit stewed in a sugar syrup, with wine, and some sort of spice, lies in adding the fruit in the right order according to its cooking time.

 For a **Compota de invierno** you need Reineta or cooking apples, pears, dried peaches or apricots, prunes, raisins, red wine and cinnamon. Put 1 litre (1¾ pints) of red wine in a stainless steel saucepan with 3 heaped tablespoons of sugar and the cinnamon. Begin by cooking the dried peaches and prunes, all of which have been soaked beforehand. These take longer to cook. Add the raisins next. When the dried fruit is almost tender add the pears and after five minutes the apples, all peeled, cored and sliced, and cook together for another ten minutes. It is important to keep the pan covered during cooking to avoid evaporation of the liquid.

All the brothers except Millán have a drink, sometimes cider, sometimes wine, with their meals. Millán gave up drinking six years ago after a strange illness which forced him to go to Pamplona to consult a medicine man. In the Basque Country tradition dies hard; the figure and the word of the medicine man still carry weight among a peasant community which may well attend the local doctor's surgery, but who, if the latter does not do what they want, or prescribe what they think suitable, opt for another solution. The medicine man in Pamplona gave him some herbs and apparently these, taken with two or three glasses of wine, made him lose his reason and health. Now, the only time he drinks is when he tastes the cider as it ferments, week by week, in the cellar during the winter months. In April, when it is almost ready, he allows his family and friends from roundabout to go down to the cellar under the house and taste the newly born cider straight from the vat. The following month he bottles it, using a small hand-operated machine to insert the corks under pressure. For the last year or so he has used plastic corks because the real ones have escalated in price. The whole production of some six hundred litres a year is drunk at Pasus, though some bottles are given away to friends and relatives.

In the olden days his grandfather and father made cider; now the apples are taken to the nearby cider-mill or *sidrería* for crushing and only the fermentation takes place in the *caserío's* cellar. 'My grandfather used to say that Pasus cider was much better than the stuff they made at the *sidrería* and I think that he was right', comments Millán. Pasus cider is very good: dry, transparent and of great character and body. It is made with the apples that one can see from Cándida's kitchen window. It is impossible to say when the varieties found today were first grown in the Basque Country, but we do know that the trees have been a common sight in the landscape since time immemorial. Indeed Herman La Chapelle, the French historian, believed that it was Basque sailors and fishermen who introduced the apple tree to Normandy, where it was unknown before the fourteenth century. We also know that the Romans wrote contemptuously about the savage people of the mountains, who had only apple juice to drink, and that by the eleventh century cider had become common currency for payment of farm rents and church tithes. Two types of *sagardoa*, naturally fermented farmhouse cider, were made at that time. One called *pitarra* was watery, made by simply crushing and macerating the apples and then adding water. The second type, true cider, was made by pressing the apple pulp, then breaking that up with a wooden mallet before pressing it again to give a cheese of dry pulp; the liquid was then poured into huge oak vats, of some five thousand litres, called *kupelas* or *kupelak*, and the must left uncovered for fifteen to twenty days for the initial tumultuous fermentation, which purified the juice. Finally, the vats were sealed for the second, gentler fermentation. This cider-making process was considered mysterious, even magical, and the moon was said to play a large part in the success or failure of the finished clear, bubbling drink. Only the second type, the true cider now called *sagardoa*, is made today. Connoisseurs say that the best is made in the lower regions of Guipúzcoa; the ciders there are pale in colour, dry and, according to them, do not lie heavily on the stomach. They should be dry, with a little acidity, though not too much, and soft on the palate. In the glass they should be almost transparent with *pétillance* or sparkle, a smell of apples, plenty of body and greenish-straw colour. The sweeter ciders made in higher regions are less sought after.

It is five o'clock, time for the afternoon snack; this time the omelettes which contain onion and parsley as well as cod, wait on the table with a generous dish of freshly sliced cold meats. To make the omelettes Cándida puts the broken-up dried cod to soak for a few hours. She uses a heavy iron frying-pan and adds a few drops of olive oil. In a bowl she breaks the eggs, two per brother, and flakes in the fish and the onion and finely chopped parsley. When the oil is hot she pours in the egg mixture which quickly sets. Cándida has the knack of making them slightly moist. Her nephew, who likes to go to the farm for the *merienda*, or teatime, always jokes that the cod must be of fresh waters because it lacks salt. Millán is cutting slices off a round one kilo loaf. On the plate there is cured ham and a rather spicy *chorizo* sausage; someone's hand must have slipped when adding the paprika powder, or *pimentón*, the day they killed the pig!

The annual *matanza*, or killing of the pig, on a Basque *caserío* takes place in November. A few days before the word goes out to the neighbours to come and help. The women arrive first thing in the morning and immediately set about chopping kilo upon kilo of onions which will be used to make the first black puddings. The house pig, unlike those which are raised to be sold, is fed on fresh vegetables and maize. 'It is most important that the animals we are going to live off should be well fed', explains Cándida.

For anyone witnessing pig-killing for the first time the event is undeniably horrific. Two men seize the animal by the legs and cut its throat. As the blood pours out one of the local women shakes it in a bucket kept for this purpose, to prevent it from coagulating. Next the animal is put to hang for several hours. At this stage the woman of the house fries the liver, which traditionally only men eat. Then the women get to work. First they make the black puddings, which in this area of Villabona also contain oregano. The onion which was finely chopped and boiled until tender first thing in the morning is now mixed together with small pieces of fat, pounded garlic, sweet and hot *pimentón*, oregano and the blood of the pig. All the women are sitting next to each other making the *morcillas*, or black puddings, pressing the mixture into the fine tripes; after this they will be boiled and hung from the ceiling. Next they prepare the *chorizo* mixture of meat, fat, *pimentón*, garlic and salt which has to macerate for twenty-four to forty-eight hours before it is ready to go into the tripes. The men are in charge of the butchering of the animal which is conducted following the rituals established since time immemorial; the hams are taken away for curing, some parts of the fats for salting and the meat which is going to be eaten fresh is cut into pieces, while the rest will go directly into the freezer. At the end of the day, presents, known as *txerrimonis*, are given to the neighbours who helped with the pig killing. They would usually consist of some black pudding, a lump of bacon and some spare ribs, all wrapped in a cabbage-leaf.

In Cándida's mother's day, once the pig had been butchered large joints of meat were stored in salt in *kutxas*, beautiful wooden chests, which nowadays fetch high prices in antique shops. Stones were placed on the top of the meat to press it as it cured. Now the days of salting pork belong to a remote past and the meat is simply frozen. Similarly, the *chorizo* sausages were stored in lard, in large earthenware jars. 'The two preserved hams last us a whole year in spite of the fact that my brothers love it and are always cutting themselves generous slices', comments Pepita.

If she is running late, sometimes Cándida prepares a recipe which was one of her mother's specialities, originally from Navarre, but now cooked all over Euskadi, particularly in the *caseríos* where food is served. All you need is a few slices of cured ham, which tends to be less salted than the Andalucian versions, and a thick tomato sauce. Cándida fries the ham slightly first and then adds the tomato sauce to the frying-pan, but in Navarre the ham is added to the tomato sauce uncooked

In spare moments Cándida also does all sorts of bottling and preserving, particularly of tomatoes and red peppers. In winter she will use the tomatoes to prepare the sauces she uses in many of her dishes.

 To make **Salsa de tomate**, tomato sauce, she adds ½ chopped onion, ½ a clove of garlic and ¼ kg (1lb) of tinned tomatoes to cold olive oil in a frying-pan and cooks for about thirty minutes or until the olive oil appears on the surface of the sauce.

Another speciality is fruit preserves, particularly those made from Reineta apples. She just peels, cores and chops the fruit and simmers it with a little water and its own weight in sugar. Once soft, she sieves the mixture and puts it into the same jars which her mother used to use. Fig preserve is also popular with her brothers.

At the end of the day, when night has fallen, the family comes back indoors once more for their few hours of relaxation. Invariably they are tired, but nonetheless it is the best part of the day. Supper is both simpler and lighter than lunch. In winter Cándida usually makes a warming soup like *porrusalda*, a truly popular Basque Country dish. It is basically a leek and potato soup to which dried salt-cod is often added, although following her traditional approach, Cándida prefers it without the fish.

 To serve four people **Porrusalda** you will need 4 leeks, 4 potatoes, 2 cloves of garlic, 1 carrot, 2 tablespoons of olive oil, water and salt. Clean the leeks well; part of the green can also be used, but I prefer to add only the white part to this particular vegetable soup, cutting it into small pieces. Peel the carrots and the potatoes and cut them up. Bring the water to boil in a medium-sized pan, add the leeks and carrots and, once the liquid returns to the boil, reduce the heat and cook slowly. Cut the garlic into thin slices. In a frying-pan heat the oil, add the garlic and cook until it is a light gold in colour. Add the potatoes once the leeks, carrots and pepper are already half cooked and after a few more minutes, the garlic and olive oil.

Their relaxation after supper is simple: good conversation around the kitchen table, perhaps some television. Lucas and José Luis often go to bed early, but Pepita and Millán always have something to consult each other about while Cándida finishes clearing away the meal. They are not in the habit of going out drinking, except for *Santiago*, Saint James' day, when they go down to the village in the evening. In the past, they used to go to the cinema in Villabona every Thursday, but there is no longer one there and they do not like the films that they show in Tolosa, so it is not worth the journey. In any case, they feel so much more at ease at home. One thing the brothers do miss, however, are the old stone hauling contests in which oxen pulling great stones race each other over short distances. Over the years their draft oxen won a clutch of silver cups which are now lined up in the glass case in the hall. 'We had a pair of champions who took first prize every year in the provincial stone hauling championship,' explains Millán proudly, 'but we had to sell them a few years ago, since then we have missed out on one of the high pleasures of life. Times change.' The only thing that they do occasionally, on a Sunday, is to go to the local *frontón* to see the *pelotaris*. Pelota is a great game and one of the national past times of the Basques. There are different types, but the *Cesta punta*, played with an elongated basket which is tied to the player's hand, is an exciting and fast game in which gambling adds to the interest. In every Basque village the *frontón* and the church go hand in hand. When the game is over, they collect the women and go out to lunch at a *caserío* that serves meals, as they do if there is something to celebrate, such as a first communion, or the annual reunion with the rest of the family. The last time they did this they had a dish of French origin, a leg of lamb with white beans, which was so delicious, that Cándida took the trouble to ask for the recipe. This dish can be made with dried or fresh beans, but if you use the latter, double the quantity.

 To prepare **Leg of lamb with white beans** for four people you need a leg of lamb weighing about 1kg (2 lbs), boned and tied up, 250 g (9 oz) of white beans, 1 green pepper, ¾ of a medium-sized onion, chopped, 2 large carrots, olive oil, garlic and salt. Put the dried beans to soak the night before, when you want to cook them put them in a saucepan with fresh water, ½ the onion, the carrots, the pepper, a good few drops of virgin olive oil and a pinch of salt. The water should cover the ingredients completely. Simmer for about two hours, adding a little cold water from time to time. Then sauté the rest of the onion **until golden brown** and add to the beans, which by now are without liquid. Next, put the lamb to roast in a moderate oven, 200°C (400°F, Gas mark 6), first having made some incisions in the skin and inserted the garlic cloves, peeled and cut into two. When the meat is done – do not allow it to dry out – remove from the oven, carve and place on a serving dish, pouring some of the juices from the roasting pan over it. Arrange the beans around it and serve immediately.

In the past celebrations were more animated. Pepita remembers how, in her mother's day, a birth was an occasion for real celebration, a fiesta known as the *Atzolorras*. Once the first three or four weeks had passed and the mother recovered her strength, she would invite her female neighbours to celebrate the new arrival. They, in their turn, would each bring a fowl as a present. There was no place here for men, except for the sole accordionist who was also the driver of the ox-cart which called to collect them, one by one, to take them to the party. They would dance and drink plenty of cider and sweet wine made from Muscatel grapes and quinine, known as *Quina San Clemente*, until they were more than merry. The celebration meal, too, was a grand affair; there were all sorts of salads, roast chicken with potatoes, and milk and apple puddings. The evening would fly with more dancing and laughter until the time came for them to return home. The accordionist drove them back in his cart on what was rather a noisy journey.

If the mother fell ill, then the milk-drawer would be called. He was a remarkable character who made a profession of attending mothers whose breasts were infected, but who needed to be able to feed their little ones, by sucking all the infection from the unfortunate woman's breast. I wonder how many candidates there must have been for the task in the locality.

Today, many of the celebrations have died out, but a *pastel vasco* or *gâteau basque* remains an essential part of any celebration. This is another recipe which is made on both sides of the Pyrenees. Wonderful large size examples are often for sale in the local markets and they are always available in the excellent cake shops, *pastelerias*, of the country.

 For a **Pastel vasco** cake you need 300 g (11 oz) of flour, 200 g (7 oz) of sugar, 2 egg yolks and 1 egg white, 200 g (7 oz) of butter, grated lemon rind, a pinch of salt and a teaspoon of yeast. For the confectioner's custard you need 250 ml (9 fl oz) of milk, 2 egg yolks, 250 g (9 oz) of flour, 50 g (2 oz) of sugar, a drop of rum and a few raisins or sultanas. First melt the butter in a pan. Put in a bowl the flour, sugar and when the sugar has dissolved remove from the heat. Beat the egg yolks with the flour and gradually add the milk, which by now should be just tepid. Return the mixture to the heat and cook carefully until it no longer tastes of flour. Allow to cool and then add the rum and raisins. Divide the dough into two and roll out each piece until it is 4mm thick. Prepare a loose-bottomed tin by brushing with a little butter to prevent sticking. Line it with the dough and fill with the custard. Cover with the other piece of pastry and brush with beaten egg. Traditionally lines are drawn across the top with a knife. Cook at 160°C (300°F, Gas mark 2), for about forty-five minutes.

The *caserío* life described in this chapter continues, though families who want to live their lives as they have until now are becoming fewer and fewer (apart from anything else women refuse to marry men destined to survive the life of a farmer). Nowadays, for a farm to be financially viable it needs to lease more land and invest in new machinery. Many of the isolated and deserted *caseríos* are now taking on a new lease of life in the hands of young families tired with city life and who seek a weekend refuge. The men will usually cultivate a small kitchen garden so that they can take fresh vegetables back to the city, while their wives grow flowers or feed the free-range chickens.

THE LIFE OF A FISHERMAN

Antonio Arrizabalaga and his wife Miren live in the little port of Ondárroa in Vizcaya, in a tall, narrow house with wrought iron balconies over-looking the banks of the inlet. From their balcony, where a canary sings in a cage, he gazes out towards his boat, moored alongside the small, double-arched stone bridge. Sometimes the boat is almost engulfed in mud, at others it floats on the green, but somewhat dirty waters of the inlet.

Although Antonio has been retired for years, he cannot give up venturing out to sea. In his small boat he fishes for squid most days, both in summer and winter. 'I catch them, I clean them and I cook them', he says proudly. He speaks Castilian slowly, like a foreign language, and occasionally his words are interspersed with one or two in Basque. When he speaks of the sea he becomes animated and his small eyes, still bright and lively in spite of the many wrinkles around them, are full of spirit and inspiration.

These days Antonio fishes just a few miles out from port, using a hook specially designed for squid. Firstly he attaches a length of very fine line and then, on top of it, a strong cord. When he casts it out to sea it is easy to tell if it has reached the bottom and reel it in a little. He knows straight away when a squid has been hooked by the slight pull and jerk on the line; usually he uses two sets of tackle at once and in very little time he catches an enormous number.

Antonio first went to sea sixty-five years ago, at the age of ten. His father, a widower with seven children whose main concern was to feed them all, found him work on a small fishing smack used mainly for catching anchovy and sardine. Twelve metres long, it was propelled by the oars of the ten crewmen. Some were old and some young, but none so young as he. They slept on a worn-out sail and rested their heads on bundles of old clothes. It was Antonio's task to remember which bundle belonged to whom; each time that he forgot he received a beating. Sometimes he also cut pilchard bait into pieces. 'We would put out to sea twice a day; at dusk, about five in the evening, to fish for two or three hours and again at dawn, with very little light. The bait attracted the fish from the sea bed so they congregated around the vessel. Then it was easy to net them, with a *boliche*, a finely meshed drag-net.' On Saturdays, once the expenses had been dealt with, the ship's steward would share out their meagre earnings among the crew.

At the age of fourteen Antonio went to work for his father, who had bought one of the small steamers which appeared in Ondárroa at the turn of the century. Until then, all Ondárroa's fishing smacks, skiffs and vessels for exporting timber, had been laboriously built in the town's own boatyards, as in every Biscay port. Their engine power, puffing out impressive clouds of smoke, promised much, but the high coal consumption was to bring ruin to more than one ship owner. The whole family used to work on the boat, yet the money they earned was barely enough to make ends meet. Antonio's father was the boss, his brother the engineer, his three sisters the netmenders. Antonio joined the crew as a sailor and was soon promoted to stoker. The rhythm of their life was dictated by the sea and the *costeras*, or traditional fishing seasons. There was no fixed time for starting, no set hour for turning the boat towards port.

In those days the whole town gained its living from the sea.

Since the fourteenth century Ondárroa had always been a town of fishermen, traders and boat-builders. The same details of daily life were repeated all over the town: large wicker baskets for carrying the fish awaited their daily routine; nets were mended and prepared with bait – hooks by the women, some young, others old, with one or two babies sleeping by their sides; old men sat in silence alone with their thoughts while old women, dressed in black, their lives almost over, handled their rosaries with tired and restless fingers, their eyes praying for salvation.

To an outsider's eyes, Ondárroa was a more attractive place in those days, its sturdy, local stone buildings several stories high, but all in scale with the narrow inlet, and with their windows gazing expectantly towards the sea. Today, as then, beyond and further inland lies the magnificent Basque landscape, the deep green of meadow and woodland rises up to the imposing peak sheltering the town and inlet, farmsteads are dotted here and there and the cemetery is perched on the highest summit. In the port, the inlet itself, alongside the Fishermen's Guild and the bridge, used to be all sorts of vessels, including skiffs and fishing smacks. When the tide was high they made a graceful picture, bobbing peacefully on the water, but when mud predominated, they lay, as though injured, on their sides, accentuating the ungainliness of the town at low tide. *Txalopaundixe*, sailing boats used for bream and tunny-fishing, *Bolintxeruk*, somewhat wider than the fishing smacks and driven by diesel engines, and various small motor vessels would be ranged in twos and threes across half the width of the inlet. Today on the town hall and bridge, you can still see the carved coats-of-arms which illustrate the history of the town: the shield of Ondárroa depicting its bridge, supporting on the one side a chapel and on the other, a castle surmounted by a crown, all guarded by a lion. Beneath the bridge is a small boat followed by a whale.

Behind this picturesque scene, life was much harder than today. Antonio has never forgotten how the rules of life were spelt out at school. On one side of the classroom sat the son of the shipyard's owner and the boy of the local doctor; on the other were the rest of the village children, who lived in permanent poverty. His sister who in her youth worked as a netmender and itinerant fish-seller, remembers more clearly the hours which she spent as a child, with her nose pressed against the window of the village bakery and the confectioner's. Their mouths would water as they gazed at the goodies on show behind the glass, apparently only a few inches from their mouths, but in reality many miles away.

Meanwhile, day after day, the *arrantzales*, or fishermen, went to sea searching for a catch on a daily, but always adventurous, routine.

In spring, when the sea dressed itself in a lighter blue and moderated its temperament, they went out fishing for anchovy. In those days, there were no sonar or sounding devices and the best method was to follow the dolphins who stirred up the fish from the sea bed. Once they could see the shoals on the surface they would throw out the net. On other occasions they would change to a finely meshed gillnet and set off in a straight line according to the direction of the wind, with the net, weighted along its bottom edge, fixed to the boat. Either way, when the shoal swam into the net they were trapped. These fish commanded, and still do, a higher price than those caught in a larger net as they were fresher when they reached the port. Once back on shore the women would come aboard wearing large waterproof aprons, and carefully pick out the fish, one by one, till they lay in glistening heaps in the basket.

As summer approached and the weather grew kinder, the boats would go out much further from the coast to fish. This was the *costera del bonito*, the Cantabrian tunny season. Also called *albacora*, this northern tunny (*Thunnus alalunga*) is quite different from *Thunnus thynnus*, which is fished on the coasts of the rest of the Peninsula, particularly in the south. Pale in colour, usually one metre long and weighing about ten kilos – *bonito* is the superior variety whether eaten fresh or canned. In Spain the housewife generally distinguishes it from ordinary tunny by the rule of thumb that the red-tinged flesh is tunny, whereas, as far as she is believed, *bonito* has white flesh. In those days, the tunny fishing rights were reserved for just a few ports – Motrico, Lekeitio, Bermeo and Ondárroa – and the prime season lasted for a month and a half between 30 June and the *Día de la Virgen*, Our Lady's Day, on

15 August. At the beginning of the season drift lines, or *currican* lines (ending in a single hook, to which pieces of maize husk were attached to resemble live fish) were used to entice the tunny. Sometimes the women even tied multi-coloured ribbons to the hooks as these were thought to produce good results. Once the boat was moving, the lines would be thrown out from two long poles or outriggers which projected from the port and starboard bow. Each was about five metres long, and with a ring at the tip through which three sets of tackle slid. When it rained the men used to wear capes treated with linseed oil, but sooner or later they would get soaked through to the skin.

The tunny-fishing season was a time of great festivities; the catch was large and every family benefited. Antonio and his sisters and brothers would then have a great annual treat: their father would take them all to Casa Paco, the town's restaurant, to have a dish of real ice cream made with eggs and with cinnamon sprinkled on top. More traditionally they ate barbecued tunny and *marmitako*, a rich fish stew which is at its most delicious in the summer when the tunny feeds voraciously, so that its flesh is rich in oil and full of flavour. Now it is renowned throughout Spain, but once it was simply a Basque fisherman's dish called after the *marmita* or stewpot.

Probably there are as many versions of *marmitako* as there are inspired sea cooks, which is a great many. Since it invariably figures in the competitions which are part of the village fiestas to celebrate the arrival of summer and is made by chefs all over the Basque Country, there are all kinds of gastronomic versions. Some of the ingredients, such as the tunny, potatoes, peppers, oil and salt, are common to all recipes, but the others vary considerably. Some cooks add dried red peppers or chilli, while other versions contain *salsa vizcaina* (see page 45), which makes it richer, or a glass of whisky or brandy. The recipe which follows comes from a little book published in Ondárroa called *La Cocina Popular Marinera*, in other words, popular seafaring cookery, which includes a selection of the recipes presented at one of the town's cookery competitions held annually early in the summer. The only condition of entry is that the recipes should be original ones, not culled from cookery magazines or books. This recipe did not win the first prize of twenty thousand pesetas, but was given special mention.

 To prepare **Marmitako** for four fishermen you need, 1 kg (2 lbs) of tunny, 1 kg (2 lbs) of potatoes, a red onion, 3 green peppers, 2 cloves of garlic, 3 tablespoons of tomato sauce, a little olive oil, water and salt. Clean the tunny well, removing skin and bones. Cut it into small chunks. In a frying-pan gently fry the onions in oil until golden-brown, together with the garlic (finely chopped). Peel the potatoes, cut them into medium-sized pieces and place them in an earthenware dish, together with the green peppers, similarly chopped. Add the fried onion to the fish and thoroughly mix everything and cover with warm water. Cook until the potatoes are almost done and then add the tunny, tomato and a little salt. Cook for a few minutes longer until the tunny is done. It is traditional to add a few slices of bread before removing from the heat.

This was also the time of *pelota* matches and regattas, held in nearly all Cantabrian ports. Here, the two sports go hand in hand at fiestas and as matters of masculine pride. A poet from Ondárroa, Luis Fernández Ardavín, wrote:

Cuando hace falta un remero	When they need an oarsman
para ganar las regatas,	To win in the regattas
Shanti acude. Agil, ligero.	Shanti will be there. Quick and agile
Usa boina y alpargatas,	Wearing a beret and espadrilles
Mueve con golpe somero,	He moves his arms
los brazos, y sin bravatas,	With a shallow stroke and no fuss,
pero seguro y certero	But safely and surely
su equipo llega el primero	His crew comes in first.
cuando hace falta un remero	When they need an oarsman
para ganar las regatas.	To win in the regattas.
Pluma leve es la pelota	When Shanti is on the pelota court
cuando Shanti va al frontón,	The ball is as light as a feather
Como blanca gaviota	Like a white seagull
vuela, salta, corre, bota	It flies, leaps, races, bounces
de la cancha al paredon	From the pitch and against the wall
Y en la viva animación	When Shanti is on the pelota court
con que el corro se alborota,	The ball is as light as a feather
pluma leve es la pelota	And the crowd cheers him on
cuando Shanti va al frontón.	With great excitement.

The regattas organized by the local committees of the various fishing ports are exciting events; not only does man strive to win his perpetual battle against the sea – in the same vessel he used to fish in not so long ago – but also he competes fiercely against his fellow fishermen. He rows, not only for himself, but also for the honour of his locality and in Basque terms, this is a great matter of pride. The excited crowd cheers them on from the shore, as the boats cut through the waves.

At day break the next day, the men would go to sea in search of fish. In the second part of the tunny season, in September, they used a different method to catch the *albacora*, spreading the net to catch anchovy, which in turn would attract tunny. The anchovy would be hauled in and then, with one of them still alive as bait on a hand held bamboo rod with a short line and a hook, they would cast within reach of the tunny and catch it with the live bait. The tunny have a habit of leaping high above the surface of the water and to prevent them from becoming aware of the fishing boat, the sea was and still is today, sprayed from the decks with great hoses which produce a camouflaging curtain of water which allays the suspicions of the magnificent fish completely. In the case of the larger fish the struggle between man and fish could be most dramatic and all sorts of wiles were necessary, such as exploiting the momentum of the fish's leap to haul it aboard. When the fish was the victor the tackle was often wrecked by being dragged down to the depths of the ocean.

Each boat had a cook who, in addition to his seafaring tasks, prepared the meals. He was paid a little extra, but not much, to do all the cooking for the season. A concrete slab, about eight inches thick, with charcoal on it and a grid over the top, served as a makeshift grill which was used twice a day, morning and evening. If they ever came across a trawler they would exchange some tunny for other fish, in order to eat something different for a change. For breakfast they would have garlic soup.

According to her family, the **garlic soup** which Antonio's sister makes, simple as it may sound, has no equal. She fries the bread cut into small, thin squares, until golden and adds cubes of cured ham. Then she puts some olive oil and chopped garlic into a *cazuela* or earthenware dish. If you do not have one, use a metal one. The fried-bread and cubes of ham are simply sautéed in the oil, covered with water and cooked for about ten minutes.

Antonio believes that when it comes to food and particularly to fish, simplicity is unbeatable. According to him, the best fish soup of all is made from *cabracho* or scorpion fish. They often used to make it at sea. 'We would put a good-sized fish to simmer in water and meanwhile, sauté a finely chopped onion in oil, until golden-brown, then we would simply add the onion to the fish, together with a little salt.'

Much of the *albacora* fish went to the canning industry, which has flourished here since the beginning of the nineteenth century, when many Italian families moved here and set up in business. Alongside the large factories able to process millions of cans a year, there were then hundreds of small, almost craft workshops, which managed as well as they could. One of these, in the town of Marquina a few kilometres from Ondárroa, is still producing all sorts of canned seafood today. The firm's name is Italian as are the majority of the canning factories of the north but its day-to-day running is in the hands of a Basque couple whose name is as old as the town they live in. Their most important products are still the most traditional; canned tuna and anchovies in olive oil. The fish, weighing up to ten kilos, are cut in half, placed in large wire baskets and boiled in salted water before skinning and boning. Then the flesh is packed by hand into tins, to make either small drums for the catering industry or miniature tins ideal for salads and omelettes, and then they are transferred to a machine which covers the fish with olive oil and seals them hermetically. Finally, large steam chambers are used in the sterilization process. Luisa, who runs the factory, says that preserving tunny at home is easier than many people think. It is, after all, the domestic recipe from which the factory version evolved.

For **Atun blanco del Cantábrico** clean the tunny well and cut into moderately thick slices. Using a large saucepan, bring plenty of salted water to the boil and simmer the fish until it almost falls off the bone. Remove it, drain, and take out the bones. Only use the white parts; the dark patches do not taste as good. Fill some Kilner jars carefully, trying to arrange the fish as neatly as possible. Then pour on enough olive oil to cover. Fasten the lids and cook in a *bain-marie* for about an hour. By using a pressure cooker you will save time. This fish remains a favourite house ingredient. In summer, quite delicious salads are made based on diced boiled potato mixed with fresh tomato, cucumber, some freshly-cooked prawns and a small tin of strips of tunny, simply dressed with the oil in which the fish was preserved, a drop of white wine vinegar and a little salt.

Sardines and anchovies are prepared too. The anchovies are often eaten laid on top of some very thin strips of roasted and then peeled red pepper, dressed with garlic and some virgin olive oil, on a slice of fresh country bread. The fishermen's wives would often preserve anchovies in salt, to serve on bread as an afternoon snack. To prepare these you need several wide-necked containers such as crocks or jars. Clean the anchovies well and remove their heads. Cover the bottom of the container with some coarse sea salt and then make layers of anchovies and salt until the jar is full. The last layer should be of salt. Then cover with a lid, if possible a wooden, tightly-fitting one, and place any sort of weight on top, even a stone will do. A few days later the lid should have sunk slightly as the salt dissolves in the blood from the fish; at this stage several more layers can be added. In order for the anchovies to be properly cured they need to be left three or four months. If they are preserved in May, which is when they are at their best, you can begin to eat the top layers in September. Lift a few out of the container and soak them in water for a few minutes, then remove their backbone and cover with the best olive oil. Preserved sardines are not as highly thought of as tunny or anchovies but they have always been seen as an important part of the seaman's diet. They can be preserved in hundreds of ways: soused (dipped in flour, fried with garlic and cooked in vinegar), in oil, or treated like the so-called 'herrings', *arenques* in Castilian, which are preserved by salting.

With winter, the Cantabrian skies are perpetually clouded and the sea darkens; at times it appears melancholic, at others, angry, almost enraged. The beaches are empty and the memory of children playing at the sea's edge almost forgotten, but the sea is beautiful, this is when she comes to life taking on her true, subtle colours as though seen through a misted glass. 'In the old days,' Antonio says, 'the life of the fishermen became hard, sometimes almost an impossible struggle.' This was the season of red bream, one of the most sought-after of the northern fish, both for Basque dishes and sale to the rest of Spain. Centuries ago, when Christmas Eve was an obligatory day of abstinence in the regions of Castile and Aragon, it gradually became the centrepiece of Catholic Spain's most meaningful religious celebration, and has kept a special meaning ever since. Before the opening of the season, the fishermen would meet together with the other members of their Guild and choose the *señeros*, three skilled sailors whose task it was to study the sea each day and indicate when the fleet should put to sea, and six *faroleros*, or lamp-lighters, who regulated the departure of the boats. The *señeros* had to rise an hour before the rest of the crew to decide if the weather conditions were suitable, and run through the streets of Ondárroa striking three blows with a club as a signal to get up. Meanwhile the *faroleros* would be collecting the red lanterns used for signalling and making sure that all the boats in the bay were ready to put to sea. This way each boat was given an equal chance of being the first to reach the fishing grounds and of taking up its position there.

The departure time for any particular day was set in advance throughout the various ports, depending on the distance to the bream-fishing grounds: if they were very far away, then the expedition might set out at midnight, if they were nearby, four or five in the morning would be early enough. Since it would be disastrous for anyone to be late on board, each ship would also pay two young women who would check that all the fishermen would be up and ready to go to sea on time. Usually, it took them little more than a quarter of an hour to stumble from their beds, dress and make their way to the port. Once all the vessels from different ports had converged at the chosen fishing area at the same hour, another lantern-keeper would give the signal for fishing to begin and the tackle would be lowered into the sea. This was designed to do the least harm to the flesh and consequently the flavour of the fish, and consisted of a number of hooks attached to fine strings knotted on to the main line which could be cast into the sea either horizontally or vertically. Each boat would cast out its lines, about fifty of them to a vessel, simultaneously and at great speed. The line would be left in the water for about two hours and then hauled in with the bream and the occasional much prized hake. Since the lines became entangled with each other at the slightest provocation, unravelling them caused many head-aches. On each boat, the catch was shared out between all. The work was so hard and the boats so crowded that the crew usually ate packed food using the hatchway, or *escotilla*, as a table. Antonio would often take *zurrukutuna*, a soup made with dried salt-cod.

 For **Zurrukutuna** for four fishermen you need 4 pieces of dried salt-cod, each about 100g (3½ oz), soaked and reconsti-tuted ready to use (see page 16), 200g (7oz) of bread (stale will do perfectly well), 4 eggs, 1 finely chopped green pepper, the flesh of 1 dried red pepper, 2 cloves of garlic, a little chilli, olive oil, salt (if required) and a drop of water. Pour the oil into an earthenware dish and add the peeled and chopped gar-lic. Fry until golden brown and then add the pieces of cod and cook until the fish has lost its gelatinous texture. Remove the cod from the heat and break it up into flakes. Add the bread to the dish in small pieces, together with the green pep-per, and sauté. Then return the fish to the pan with the red pepper and the water. Leave to simmer for a while. Lastly add the chilli. When it is nearly done, break the eggs into the dish and allow to poach before serving.

The *besugo*, or sea bream, was rarely cooked on board due to the regular bad weather conditions and the lack of time. The most popular way of cooking bream is, *a la Donostiarra* meaning prepared in the San Sebastián style, grilled over charcoal made, if possible, from the holm oak tree. The grand masters of Basque cooking lay great emphasis on due care in the preparation stage. For **Besugo a la donostiarra** the fish must be very fresh. Once it has been cleaned, it is sprinkled with salt and hung up for a few hours. About an hour before the meal, it is brushed with a little oil, (traditionally this was, and often still is, done with a chicken's feather) and placed over the coals. The grilling is most simply done using a fish-clamp made of wire of the sort that Basque *asadores*, barbecue restaurants, often use to make turning easy. When the skin is well browned and the flesh well cooked on both sides, a little olive oil is heated together with two or three peeled and sliced cloves of garlic. Just before the garlic becomes brown, this is all poured over the fish, which has previously been slit open and boned. Another traditional way of serving the fish is *a la espalda*, on its back, when it is boned before cooking and grilled opened flat, with garlic and a little chilli. Other fish, like monkfish, are also delicious cooked in this way.

At home, the cooking was done by Antonio's sisters, even when they were little more than children, using the limited ingredients that they could find or buy cheaply during each fishing season. Their cooking has changed little over the years, and today they make many of the same dishes, although they are more sophisticated versions. Among them, tunny fish casserole, tunny fish balls and baked bream, all traditional Basque dishes, remain favourites.

 To prepare **Bonito en cazuela** you need for four people 1 kg (2 lbs) of tunny, ½ kg (1 lb) peeled and chopped tomatoes, 4 chopped onions, 100 ml (3½ fl oz) of olive oil, a little sugar and salt. Soften the onion in the oil in an earthenware casserole; when it is translucent add the tomato and salt and cook on a low heat for one hour. Sieve and put half the mixture into the dish with the slices of fish on top and shake the dish gently backwards and forwards over the heat. Then pour over the rest of the tomato sauce and cook on a slow heat until the tunny is tender and comes away from the bones easily. This dish can also be prepared with the fish previously coated in flour.

 Albóndigas de bonito made from minced fish are very tasty. For four people you need 1 kg (2 lb) of tunny, skinned, boned and finely chopped, 1 litre (1¾ pint) of fish stock, 3 large onions, 4 eggs, some stale bread (crust removed) soaked in a little milk, 2 tablespoons of olive oil, chopped parsley and 2 chopped cloves of garlic. For the sauce you need 1 glass of white wine, the juice of ½ lemon, a large knob of butter, 3 dessertspoons of flour and a little fish stock. Finely chop the onions and lightly fry in olive oil in an earthenware casserole on a low heat until golden brown. In a bowl combine the tunny, garlic, parsley, bread, onion and 3 of the eggs which have been well beaten, to form a paste. Scoop up a spoonful of the mixture and form it into a small ball with your hands. Dust with flour, coat with the remaining egg, beaten well, and fry in olive oil until golden brown. These fishballs can be served with various sauces. Antonio's youngest sister reduces a glass of white wine and the juice of half a lemon by heating briskly. In a pan melt a knob of butter, add some finely chopped onion and about a dessertspoon of flour to thicken. Stir well then remove from the heat to cool a little. Return to the stove and add the reduced wine, a little at a time, and a little fish stock to form a light sauce. Pour into the earthenware dish on the stove to cook for a while.

 Besugo al horno, baked sea bream, once a luxury for the family, is now a more frequent winter dish. A bream of about 1 kg will feed two to three people. For this you need 3 dessertspoons of olive oil, lemon juice, 2 cloves of garlic, a little parsley and ½ glass of dry white wine. Clean the fish well, but leave the backbone in. Put all the raw ingredients in an earthenware dish in a moderate oven. Twenty minutes cooking time is usually enough. In some versions of baked bream a form of paste, almost a crust, made of breadcrumbs, a little onion, garlic and parsley, is used to cover the fish before putting it into the oven and cooking as before.

Although the life of the fishermen was very harsh, in many respects, the women's was even harder. The possibility of being widowed before forty was a very real one. The women and the old people spent much time worrying each day, as the fragile vessels daily fought their battle for survival on a sea notorious for its ill-temper and capricious moods; it was only when they finally saw the figure of their loved one disembark safely that their spirits rose again. Once the men were back in port they left everything, such as the children's education and the household expenditure, to their wives. Then was the time to enjoy *unos chiquitos*, a few glasses of wine, in the bar with their friends. Money was scarce, but there was always the odd copper or two for that particular moment.

The wife was responsible for everything including the family's finances as well as the traditional tasks which always fell to her. In winter, for example, they laboriously attached the bait for bream by hand, working from one hook to the next. The bait, usually anchovies caught at the end of the tunny fishing season, would be collected each day from the shipowner's cellar, where it was kept in barrels, covered in salt and bay leaves and prepared beforehand by the women and children. In some ways, it was pleasant work, because they could stay inside, sitting around the kitchen table, laughing, telling stories, and singing as their fingers incessantly worked away. But since each line might hold up to two hundred hooks and each fisherman would control four or five lines, it was in truth a painstaking task.

The money which from time to time might come to the family when a catch was shared out, was barely enough to live on. Many of the women would go out every day, selling the fish from great wicker baskets, often covering more than forty kilometres on foot on the journey there and back; their earnings were pitiful, but their families needed every peseta to survive. Nowadays itinerant fish sellers are a thing of the past. Nevertheless, the figure of the sardine seller from Santurce, the seaport of Bilbao, who was romanticized in the old folksongs, remains a testimony to the harshness of women's life.

Sardines were another important part of the family's diet. The Basques have never looked down on these fish simply because they are small, bony and rather cheap. Sardines fresh from the sea, simply grilled over hot coals and eaten outside a café or some beach during the summer months, are considered a delicacy. The great Spanish writer, Julio Camba, described them perfectly, 'It is not merely a dish which one shares with good company. Not a dish for eating at home with the virtuous mother of one's children, but for sharing when out with one's loose and outrageous mistress. . .'

Anchovies too, which contrary to popular belief do not belong to the sardine family, are highly rated. One frequently hears the comment that if anchovies were as scarce as elvers then they would command similarly high prices and Antonio's sister believes that they are probably the single most popular fish in Ondárroa, whether eaten fresh, soused in vinegar or canned. Not so long ago, they were so plentiful that they were used for fertilizing vegetable plots. Greeny or blue in colour with a very slim, elongated body, they are usually sold under the name *boquerones*, a reference to their enormous mouth or *boca*, they are at their best simply dipped in egg and flour, then fried, either in groups of three or four with their tails stuck together or just singly. The best known regional dish, however is *al pil-pil*, filleted and cooked in an earthenware dish in warm olive oil with plenty of slices of garlic and a piece of chilli.

In Ondárroa, the method is slightly different. To make **Anchoas al pil-pil** according to this recipe the fish must be cleaned well first, then filleted in salted water so the flesh loosens from the spine, seasoned and coated in flour. In an earthenware dish put a little olive oil to heat, add garlic and a little chilli powder and cook until golden. Put the anchovies on top with a little chopped parsley. Leave to cook for a minute or two and then turn them over. As a finishing touch you can add a drop of white wine or sherry. Cover the casserole and leave the dish to cook for three or four minutes more. In dishes of this type it is usual to allow a dozen anchovies per person. The secret lies in using really fresh fish.

Antonio's favourite dish is **Anchoas al papel**, anchovies in a parcel, a recipe which is also popular in the gastronomic competitions held in Ondárroa. To prepare these anchovies you need 1 kg (2 lbs) anchovies, with heads and backbones removed, 250 g (9 oz) mushrooms, 1 large onion, 2 cloves of garlic (peeled and chopped), a drop of lemon juice, olive oil, 1 glass of white wine, a little parsley and 150 g (5 oz) of butter. Put the finely chopped onion and the garlic in an earthenware dish with a little olive oil and cook over a low heat until golden brown. Add the sliced mushrooms and cook for ten minutes longer, without turning up the heat. Then put in the parsley, finely chopped, the white wine and the lemon juice. Next add the butter, allow to melt and then remove the casserole from the heat. Prepare 8 small pieces of greaseproof paper. Place a few anchovies on each with a little sauce on top. Fold into small parcels and put into a moderate oven for five to ten minutes.

Sometimes in the little market near the stone bridge, which the Ondárroan housewives visit every day, little baskets of red mullet are also to be found. Antonio cooks them in the following way.

 To prepare **Salmonetes al horno** you need 2-3 mullet per person, olive oil, a little butter, 3 tomatoes, 2 cloves of garlic, 1 lemon, parsley, breadcrumbs and salt. He puts the olive oil in a baking dish and then the mullet, having cleaned and seasoned them first. He makes some small incisions in each fish and puts half a slice of lemon in each. He adds 1 chopped clove of garlic, some chopped parsley and a little melted butter. Then he arranges some slices of tomato on each fish and, on top of this, a little more garlic, parsley and butter; then sprinkles with breadcrumbs and places the baking dish in the oven for about forty minutes at a moderate temperature.

This morning Antonio has been out fishing once more and this time he has brought back a basket of squid which he is now patiently cleaning at the kitchen sink. Firstly he separates the head and tentacles and the little side fins. He removes the silvery sac which contain the ink and sets it aside in a cap. Next he pulls off the very thin rather dark coloured skin, so that it becomes possible to turn the main body of the squid inside out; it is simply a matter of pushing the tip with his index finger and gradually the creature's flesh adapts itself to the shape of the finger. This achieves two things, once they have been filled with the stuffing and are fried they shrink slightly and close, preventing the filling from leaking out, secondly, and very importantly, it allows one to clean each squid thoroughly.

By now he has put all the squid, some fifty or sixty of them, on a plate. If they cannot all be eaten he will freeze some when they are prepared. He uses the legs, fins and other oddments to make a stuffing with which he then fills each squid, using a teaspoon. He puts them in an earthenware dish, adds half a medium-sized onion, finely chopped, a peeled and chopped carrot and three peeled and chopped cloves of garlic; he lightly pours a little olive oil over it all and cooks them until they are tender which takes little time as the *chipirones*, or baby squid, are small. Next he lifts out the squid one by one and transfers them to another dish; he sieves the other ingredients to form a thick sauce which he pours over the squid. Now comes the moment to add the ink, which he has diluted with a little water. He removes the ink sacs and pours the liquid into the casserole. Many Basque cooks add a little tomato, but the more orthodox reject his idea or even Antonio's additional carrots. (Personally, I do not use carrots or garlic either since for me they alter the flavour; at home we have always eaten squid cooked in the simplest way.) The old sea dog glances at the dish of squid which he has just put on the table and humorously remarks: 'Whoever would have thought when I was a lad going out drinking with my mates that in my old age I should be a cookery fanatic.' He pours red wine in the glasses and cuts some slices of bread, the best of the dish is the sauce, of course!

Antonio was married with his own young family to support when he joined the crew of a small deep-water trawler. His father had decided to sell his fishing boat and left Antonio with no means of financial support. The only work that was easy to find was on the new purpose-built trawlers, which could carry enough fuel for journeys of several weeks and venture much further out to sea in search of species which were not to be found around the Iberian continental shelf and new grounds where they could fish for traditional catches such as bream and hake. They would put to sea for eight to ten days at a time and normally they would continue fishing until they were hit by a storm. In those days the trawlers had no modern equipment. Two boats would trawl the net, which would sink right down to the sea bed since it had a number of chains attached to it. They would often catch as many as twenty different species, even though the mesh was large; everything from anchovy swimming near the surface to large hake. On the deep-water vessels the fishermen classified and reclassified the fish, packing it into wooden boxes graded according to size, washing it down with a hose and then storing it in ice in the holds. During the summer they worked eighteen hours a day, though the seafarers could rest rather more in winter. So unremitting was the work that most of the time the cook would take their meals to them at their post, in a lunchbox. In this strange setting, standing between wooden cases in the hold, they would eat the best varieties of fish: turbot, hake and as many *langostinos*, large prawns, as they wished. It was traditional to fill jars with *langostinos* and vinegar and a little oil and keep them to eat at home as soon as possible at a suitable festive occasion. Turbot is still one of Antonio's wife's favourite fish. This is the way he likes to cook it.

 Before preparing **Rodaballo al txakolí con pimientos verdes**, turbot with *txakolí* and green peppers, Antonio cleans the fish thoroughly in sea water and then hangs it up in the kitchen for four or five hours to dry in a special place that he has for the purpose. For two people he uses a turbot of about 1 kg (2 lbs), 2 tablespoons of olive oil, 1 small onion, 1 clove of garlic and ½ a green pepper and half a glass of white *txakolí* wine. He begins by putting an earthenware casserole on the stove, with the oil, onion and green pepper, all finely chopped. After cooking this for ten minutes he liquidizes the mixture. Then in another earthenware dish he puts the fish, cut into several pieces, and the sauce he has just made. He leaves this to cook for about ten minutes and then turns over the pieces of fish and shakes the dish gently. After a few more minutes he adds the *txakolí*. The shaking of the dish causes the gelatine to run out of the fish and thickens the sauce. He leaves it to cook two or three minutes longer before serving.

Deep-sea fishing far from the home port, known as *pesca de altura*, was not entirely new in the Basque Country, since for centuries the cod-fishing fleet had been sailing north, loaded with salt so that their catch would not deteriorate before they reached home. This was perhaps the most demanding work of all (even compared to the long journey to the New World which was made in steam driven trawlers), since it took the fishermen away from their families for over six months of the year. The large heavy vessels, painted blue, red and green, each carrying a crew of two dozen men and two hundred and fifty tonnes of salt, would sail once the Christmas celebrations were over, the crew bidding farewell to their families until June. Of the two hundred days that these ships spent far from the Basque coast they were at sea ninety per cent of the time, put under conditions of extreme deprivation, such as shortage of fuel or foodstuffs. The voyage to Newfoundland alone took eighteen days' sailing and there was little to occupy the men meanwhile. Sometimes, when a storm raged for two to three weeks, they would feel close to despair, cooped up in the confines of the boat with little to do but play cards and get on each other's nerves. Worst of all was the monotony of life on board, day in and day out, for months on end. The shipowner knew that if the men were unhappy this would be reflected in their work and, more important still, in the cod-fishing, but there were few ways to relieve the boredom. Good food and drink were the men's only real pleasures and during the course of the long journeys, life revolved around the galley to the extent that it was almost as important to the success of the journey as the engine-room. Meals helped to give a sense of time, to break up the day and provide some comfort and luxury. The harshness of life at sea demands good food and drink, as do the low temperatures of the North American coast.

The ship would come to life at about seven o'clock each morning to a simple breakfast of bread and coffee or hot chocolate. For the first three or four days at sea they ate the fresh bread which had been taken on board at Pasajes; afterwards it had to be baked in the galley daily. On days when no work was to be done the main meal would be served at one o'clock, after the basic ship's tasks were completed. It always consisted of a stew, which might be of haricot beans, chickpeas with pig ears or simply *caldeirada*, a fish stew with potatoes. Traditionally the crews were made up of Galicians from the north-west and Basques and the former have always strongly favoured flavoured dishes; all the food on board tended to be rather over seasoned.

 Caldeirada can be made with a multitude of varieties of fish. To make this excellent sea stew, boil some sliced potatoes in sea water and when they are nearly cooked add pieces of different fish, including one or two heads to give flavour. Once everything is well cooked drain the liquid off and reserve the potatoes and fish, *la caldeirada*. In another pan fry some finely-chopped onion and cloves of garlic in olive oil; when the onion is soft and slightly coloured add a drip of vinegar and a teaspoon of paprika. This fried mixture should be poured over the potato and fish and served in a bowl.

There were two mess-rooms on board, one for the three officers and another for the men, and the line between the two was never traversed by either group. In the men's mess room long hours were spent talking, exchanging stories and wishing away the empty days.

By the time the vessels finally weighed anchor in the traditional fishing grounds the nets and equipment would have been prepared. The vessels worked in pairs to fish the cod; the first would throw out its net and trawl for about six hours, long hours of idleness and waiting, then the other trawler would repeat the procedure. The moment of truth came when the tackle was hauled back on board, bringing with it thousands of fish, some live, others already dead. Those were the days of plenty when the nets were invariably raised full of magnificent, healthy fish; nowadays, things are very different owing to the scarcity of fish and Spain losing the right to fish in the traditional waters.

From the moment that the fish were landed on the decks, the ship was ceaselessly busy until they had all been cleaned and stored in salt in the hold. Large, long wooden tables were lined up along the middle of the deck with the crew working along either side in such a way that they formed a human work-chain. Different men specialized in the various stages of cleaning and salting the fish. Some, working on the deck, would cut off the heads, others split open the fish and remove the spine, the next clean the stomach. Cod is a very delicate fish and if it has eaten a lot and is not processed quickly, its quality suffers. Since the advent, in the seventies, of very specialized German machinery most of these tasks can be performed in seconds so that the hardest part of the job falls to those who work in the salting chambers; nonetheless in the past a kind of battle used to take place between the crew on deck and those below in the hold. The greatest responsibility lay with the Master Salter who worked in the salting chamber. If he was not selective enough in deciding which fish was good enough for salting and which should be thrown back into the sea, the ship's holds would have been soon full of substandard merchandise. He and his assistants would lay down a first layer of salt, carefully placing the open fish on it, and continue adding layers of salt and fish until the pile was nearly three foot high, at which point some pieces of sacking would be stretched over the heaps to hold the pile in place during the return voyage. Eventually, as the piles were stacked up, tightly packed one on top of the other like bales of straw in a barn, they would fill almost every inch of space in the hold. Stacking was also a skilled task. If it was incorrectly done the salt dissolved and was absorbed by the fish, creating spaces when it was already too late to go back for more fish, and many problems later with balancing the packing of the cargo.

While fishing was taking place, coffee would be available continuously, day and night. The assistant cook would ring the galley bell to announce each freshly brewed pot of coffee, cut half and half coffee and Spanish brandy. If that was not enough, often he added a little more.

On working days the crew would not get below to the mess-room until about ten o'clock for breakfast, a substantial meal of ham, eggs, tinned mussels and fresh fruit. Lunch, four hours later, would be soup and meat with potatoes or fish in breadcrumbs, followed by fresh fruit. Then they would return to work until dinner, often a casserole or omelette. The only things they really lacked or missed were fresh milk and vegetables, which produced skin problems among the crew.

If the trawler found itself a real ship's cook, willing to exert himself for the sake of others, then life became much more pleasant for everyone. Some special culinary treat regularly, say once or twice a week, helped preserve their sense of time, which is apt to be lost on a vessel that spends so long at sea. One of the most popular treats easily made from store-cupboard ingredients was **buñuelos** (fritters), filled with confectioner's custard, which the cook would take to the crew with large cups of warming hot chocolate.

To prepare the **Buñuelos**, for the dough you need 75 g (2 ½ oz) of flour, 2 eggs, 100 ml (3 ½ fl oz) milk, 25 g (1 oz) butter, brandy, ¼ litre (9 fl oz) of oil, grated lemon rind, dried yeast and a pinch of salt.

For the confectioner's custard you need 2 eggs, 75 g (2 ½ oz) flour, ½ litre (18 fl oz) of milk, 75 g (2 ½ oz) of sugar, 25 g (1 oz) of butter and a little lemon rind. Make the dough first. Put the milk, butter and brandy, sugar, a pinch of salt and grated lemon rind in a saucepan. Bring to the boil and add the flour, all at the same time. Stir with a wooden spoon until the mixture comes away from the side of the pan. Allow to cool. Add the first egg and incorporate into the mixture followed by the second. When it is well beaten in add the yeast and form the mixture into little balls, using two spoons. Then heat the oil in a frying-pan and when it is really hot begin to put in the little balls of dough. Cook until they have swollen to twice their original size and are golden brown. Put them on some absorbent paper to drain off the excess oil. Using a pair of scissors cut a slit in each, in order to fill them with the confectioner's custard, which is made as follows. Beat the eggs well together with the sugar, add the flour mixed to a paste with a little cold milk. Heat the remainder of the milk in a saucepan and when it comes to the boil stir into the flour and egg mixture. Cook for five to seven minutes to ensure that the flour is cooked. Remove from the heat and mix in the butter. Allow to cool. Using either a forcing bag or a coffee-spoon fill the *buñuelos* one by one and then sprinkle them with icing sugar.

By the time the boat was ready to turn for home, the men would be exhausted from constant work and little sleep. During the long voyage back the crew used to have a couple of hours siesta after the midday meal, after which they would work another two hours around the ship until supper at about seven o'clock. After supper they would play cards and drink to fill the long hours. For some men alcohol became a real problem. Demoralization, boredom, separation from their families, the petty disagreements between crew members – the answer to all these was to have another drink.

Sometimes, at the end of a long evening, the men would make a last visit to the galley before going to bed. By then the cook had gone and it was their opportunity to show off their culinary powers to each other. Traditionally many of the crew members were Galicians, who would make seafood omelettes or *empanada*, a rich pie with a fish filling. It is always based on a sautéed mixture of chopped onion and parsley with a fish as the main ingredient, be it tunny, lamprey, eel or sardine. These pies are often to be found in Basque bars.

To prepare the pastry for the **Empanada** put ¾ kg (1 lb 10 oz) of very fine flour in a bowl with a little dried yeast. Mix well. In a saucepan heat a small glass of dry white wine with a pinch of salt, then add a tablespoon of margarine (traditionally lard was used). When the fat has dissolved completely add the flour and yeast, stirring with a wooden spoon. When the dough falls off the spoon it is ready. Leave to stand for two hours, then roll out on a cold, lightly floured surface. Usually it is rolled out in a square and the ends folded inwards several times in the same way as for flaky pastry; this operation is repeated four or five times. Cut the pastry into two. Roll out one piece until it is 1.5 cm (½ inch) thick – this is considered to be just right for the *empanada*. Spread with the chosen filling and then cover with the second piece of pastry, which should be rolled out a little thinner, so that the filling does not leak out during cooking, fold back the edges, ensuring that those of the bottom piece of pastry seal the top ones. Make a slit in the centre for the steam to escape and bake until golden brown.

To make a tunny fish filling sauté 2 large, finely chopped onions. Add thick, homemade tomato sauce and some pieces of tinned red pepper. The tunny can be fresh or canned; if you are using fresh this should be simmered in water with a bay leaf first, afterwards stir the fish, already broken into small pieces, into the tomato and onion mixture.

Eventually the ship would put into port again at Pasaies in the Basque Country. The vessels remained out at sea for weeks or months on end, processing large quantities of fish which they either froze or chilled in ice. Antonio never went to North America, although he travelled several times for the tunny fishing season to East Africa and around the Canary Islands where the weather at least was better.

The life of the fishing village has changed a great deal during Antonio's lifetime. Putting to sea has become less and less a question of men's resources and now relies instead on the capacity of the shipowner to equip his vessels with new technology: sounding devices, sonar and all kinds of other navigational aids. For the tunny fishing, for example, great tanks are used to keep alive small fish while the ship sets off in search of the shoals of tunny. The seasons have changed considerably too. Although few people from Ondárroa still fish for sea bream in winter, the tunny season is very much alive. Now, however, the fishermen prefer May for anchovy and the September tunny expeditions continue almost until Christmas in the Canary Islands. The great deep-water ships can stay at sea for months as they freeze their catch. These trawlers catch the tunny at an amazing speed, so that it can be a lucrative enterprise if they find a large shoal, for which they are prepared to go to the southern seas of the African coast. Today the Ondárroan deep-water fleet numbers ninety-five trawlers. With a total catch of two million kilos a year it is one of the most important deep-water trawler ports. On the other hand the shallow-water fleet is gradually losing its importance. Nowadays the fishermen no longer wear the old capes treated with linseed oil as today such garments are made from rubber or plastic, but although they do not get soaked to the skin as they used to, the great drawback is that the new fabrics do not breathe.

On land too, the industry has moved on to quite a different scale. The old Ondárroa market, with its wicker baskets and long stone tables, has long gone. Now a wholesale market famous for its shrewd auctioning of the catch, the bargain-making of its ship-owners and distribution to the whole of Spain, is run from a specialized office with a sophisticated intelligence system. There are two kinds of auction, one for the deep-water catch and one for the shallow. The nerve-centre of both, where all the deals are struck, is a single room with some thirty or forty traders. Even before a ship comes into port, they know whether the catch is of a high quality or not and, more important still, how long it has been lying in the holds. The traders must concentrate all the time: the slightest distraction and the lot which is being auctioned at that moment will be lost. Hour by hour they follow market prices. The particular fishing zone where the catch was made is also of crucial importance; whereas the hake which is trawled in the fishing grounds off France may make 750 pesetas a kilo, that caught in the Grand Sole grounds off Bristol might only reach 560 pesetas. Fish caught with a rod and line fetch the very best prices.

The scale of the canning industry has also changed. There is little room in the competitive open market of Europe for small, fragile firms who find it difficult to compete with the much larger ones, let alone those of the other Community countries. Gradually these small industries are disappearing from the fish-canning map of the Cantabrian Coast.

To Antonio, it is another world. 'Nowadays it is a different story', he says. 'Fishermen can become rich men and the ships are like five star hotels, only the sea remains the same.' Life has changed enormously, but he maintains that the change suits him; nowadays whatever they may say, people are better off and life is much more comfortable. He recognizes that he is growing old and contents himself with the thought of going out in his little motor-launch just a few hundred metres from the beach, from where he can almost make out his own balcony. As he sits in his small boat, his eyes scan the seas tirelessly for the glimmer of the silvery fish swimming near the surface. For at heart, he still hankers for the open sea. He says that the day when he no longer goes out to sea will be the day that he dies.

THE TRADITION OF THE KAIKU-MAKER

The Batzan valley, lost amongst the foothills of the Pyrenees, in northern-east Navarre, remains a world apart. Here, in quiet villages and isolated *caseríos*, or farmsteads, a way of life forgotten elsewhere has been preserved and events outside the valley's gently peaked horizon, even in the neighbouring Basque lowlands, are spoken of as 'what happens down there, beyond the mountains'. For the most part, the valley is clothed in an intense green; at other times in the golds and rusts of autumn. In winter snow blankets and camouflages the contours of the mountains, here tempered into gentle hills. Wild horses, sheep and goats graze on its rich pastureland.

Nestled in the valley and round about it are small, picturesque towns of sturdy houses. Here, the *caseríos* are not always lonely and remote from each other as in other Basque provinces; they stand alongside other substantial buildings with several floors, built in stone and timber, with double pitched-roofs and in the historic part of each village which dwells in the shadow of the church bell-tower. Great stone coats of arms on their facades recall adventures, triumphs and misfortunes.

In the heart of the valley, near the border with France – defined by the arbitrary decision of men who live elsewhere – lies Errazu, a Basque-Navarrese village. Here lives Domingo Echandi, the *kaik-ugileak*, or man who makes *kaikus*, scoop-shaped wooden milking pitchers. Once they were made in many places in the Basque Country, but the work is too hard for today's taste and these days the number of *kaikugileuks* can be counted on one hand.

Domingo is a small wiry man. He wears a beret, blue apron and black esparto-grass slippers; his hands are large and suntanned. Most of his working days have been spent in a sawmill and he began to work as a woodturner only in his spare time. Since his retirement he has been able to give all his time to *kaiku* making. Such is his dedication that he has now even given up social pleasures, like meeting his friends for a Saturday evening drink, to make the time he needs for his work.

Domingo, his wife Nunchi and their German shepherd dog, who answers to the name Canela, meaning cinnamon, live in a white *caserío* built faithfully in the local architectural style. On the first floor, at the top of a carved wooden staircase, are the living quarters: a large main room with a great open fireplace and a chiming clock accompanying the sound of the crackling logs burning in the grate. Leading directly off it, there is a tiny, well equipped modern kitchen. This part of the house is Nunchi's domain. Calm but quick witted and worldly, she personifies Basque matriarchy. According to her, men are just a little the superior species; they are stronger physically and the problem is that for centuries women have allowed them to lead. But it is she who runs the house and the family economy. Domingo has never set foot inside a bank, nor does he know the colour of the saving cards in his wife's charge. His life is centred around his workshop, a spacious room, with large windows which give good working light throughout the daytime hours. He opens the door to it with the pride of a man who knows that his skills will be appreciated. In the centre is a large table where the pieces are finished. On the wall hang tools, each in its place. Originally Domingo had no tools because they no longer existed for this kind of woodwork, but over the years he has ingeniously designed and made everything he needs.

Some are traditional such as the chisels, (*zintzelak*), hammers (*mazuak*), compasses (*zurgin-konpas*), and saws, but others are his own invention.

In front of the workshop, protected by a heavy waterproof canvas sheet from the sun, rain and, above all, the wind, are stored various lengths of birchwood which is used for making the utensils. Domingo explains that cut while it is still young, it has all the right qualities for crafting. More important still, it will not crack if heated, and contains none of the pigments which taint foodstuffs with strange flavours. During the winter months, with the help of several friends, Domingo fells the chosen birch trees. Sometimes he buys them from private estates, at others he obtains the necessary permission to cut down trees in the common woodland surrounding Errazu. The date and place of the felling are agreed in the village ciderhouse, which serves at one and the same time as grocery and wine shop. On this occasion Domingo will pay for all the cider he and his friends drink as they arrange the final details and play a few games of dominoes on the single, square, marble-topped bar-table. Early the next morning they go to the hills to begin the felling. The woodland vegetation is luxuriant; the birches, pines and chestnuts grow beside narrow streams of rushing, sparkling water whose continual murmur is a reassuring presence. Until a few years ago Domingo and his friends used the axe for felling the birches, but now they have power saws which cut quickly and precisely. Once the tree is felled they remove the side branches from the trunk and Domingo makes his preliminary calculations; they will cut as many times as are necessary for the required number of *kaikus* and other utensils. Gradually the lengths of wood are stacked on the trailer which, drawn by a tractor, will slowly wend its way back to the village.

Domingo works ceaselessly during the week following the timber felling; the wood must be turned speedily before it rots. He places a piece of timber on his work-bench. Using a compass he draws a circle on to the cut surface which will serve as his starting point, and does the same with the part which will be the handle, all on the same piece. Then, with great patience and strength, he begins to hollow out the centre of the wood. Once the hole is deep enough he inserts the drill into it together with a *goilareak*, an elongated scoop with a cutting edge. The task will last for hours and, once started, it cannot be stopped, as the precious single piece of wood is vulnerable at this stage. Little by little the *kaiku* takes the shape of a scoop-shaped pitcher. Next, using the *marruza*, a curved knife, Domingo gradually shapes the outside of the vessel; the handle is also completed and nothing remains but to smooth the wood with sandpaper. Three long and exhausting days have passed since he outlined the circle.

The finished *kaikus* are used mainly for milking, their shape, particularly the angled handles, allowing them to be carried with one hand. They have been used in this way for centuries since milk and dairy products have always been crucial to the valley economy. Nowadays few families rely on this kind of cottage industry. Instead the surplus milk is sold to the central dairy where cheese is produced on a larger scale in a more mechanized fashion. But some families make enough for their own requirements and the shepherd still makes sheep's milk cheese with which to supplement his earnings from livestock sales.

The *kaiku* is also used for heating milk with hot stones, an ancient method which can be traced back to prehistoric times. Then, long before the discovery of earthenware cooking pots, the inhabitants of Euskalherria filled *kaikus* with water and cooked food in them. The custom has survived using round pebbles called *kaikuarri* in Basque, collected from the river, because they add a delicious burnt taste to the milk, called *Errausana*. The *kaikuarris* are removed from the hearth using large metal or wooden tongs, and once the ash has been cleaned off with a little hot water, they are put into the *kaiku*. If the stones have become polished through constant use, when they are removed from the fire they emerge so clean that rinsing is unnecessary. Sometimes a little sugar is sprinkled on the hot stones to add a caramelized flavour. The hot milk is also used for making *mamia*, a delicious local junket. Traditionally, this delicacy was seasonal, made between the months of January and June with lamb's rennet, but now it is made all year round and most people use vegetable rennet, which you can buy in small glass jars at the village shop. It is eaten on its own, with a little honey or apple preserve or, in summer, with fresh fruit: peaches, nectarines, wild strawberries or, best of all, fat black cherries are my favourite. The fruit can also be added to the junket itself.

 To make **Mamia** with fruit you need some small moulds. Locally, these might be the smallest size of *kaiku* or the little straight-sided wooden cups called *oporra*, also used for drinking milk, or any mould available, glass or ceramic. In the base of the mould put the fruit, either fresh or gently stewed in the oven with a little sugar, cinnamon and a drop of orange liqueur. Pour over some milk which has been brought to the boil and then allowed to cool until tepid and to which a little vegetable rennet has been added. Leave in a cool place so that the curds will set around the fruit.

The other utensils Domingo makes are primarily for traditional cheesemaking. Each valley's cheese production is slightly different. Nearby, in the Roncal valley some of the best hard cheeses of the Peninsula are made from the milk of Rasa sheep: slightly dry, they have a compulsive flavour and texture. In the Batzan valley, by contrast, the *caserío* cheesemakers and shepherds make a white creamy cheese using milk produced by the Latxa breed. It is at its best eaten young, any time after four months, and before a year has expired.

Nunchi makes her cheese by hand using Domingo's utensils. Early in the morning, she hooks an *idaztia*, a funnel for straining the warm milk, usually lined with nettle leaves to remove any impurities, on to an *abatza*, a pail with two handles into which the milk filters. After all the milk has filtered through she adds a little rennet and leaves the mixture to stand for half an hour before beating it well with the *malatza*, or stirring-spoon. Once the curds have separated from the whey, she gathers them up in her hands and puts them into a *zumitza*, a cylindrical mould with holes in the bottom, which is left to drain over a small board or *kartola*. The base of the mould is carved so that the finished cheese, unmoulded and salted that evening, is patterned on the top, perhaps with a geometric combination of triangular and quadrilateral shapes or overlapping rings. The cheese is then put to dry and to mature for three to four months. Nunchi sells some of the cheese direct from the house, but she and Domingo eat much of it themselves. The older cheese, matured for nearly a year, can be used for cooking, for example in this delicious onion soup.

 To make **Sopa de cebolla** for six people Nunchi uses ½ kg (1 lb) of bread, 3 onions, 3 tablespoons of grated cheese, 150 ml (5 fl oz) of olive oil, 1¾ litres (3 pints) of water and a little salt. First she cuts the onions in julienne strips and heats water in a saucepan or kettle. Next she places an earthenware pot on a low heat, pours in the oil and adds the onion, sweating it until slightly coloured. Then the bread, cut into thin slices, is browned in the oil, and the salt and the hot water added. She turns up the heat a little until the liquid comes to the boil, then reduces it to a simmer and leaves it for about three quarters of an hour. At this stage she floats the cheese on top and puts the pot in a moderate hot oven, 200°C (400°F, Gas mark 6) for five to ten minutes to brown.

Nunchi's favourite way of eating a smooth, slightly creamy cheese is to toast small pieces over the embers until they melt and then lay them on rough country bread or, more traditionally, inside *talos*, a kind of hollow maize cake. When she was a child *talos* were an everyday dish, made from necessity. Wheat, a scarce crop in northern Spain, was expensive and bread something of a luxury, baked by each family only once a week. The rest of the week maize flour, ground at the local mill and sifted at home to remove the bran, was made into an indigestible unleavened bread or, far more appetizing and fondly remembered, these *talos*. The secret is to make them very thin so that the mixture cooks all the way through: when you cut them open the inside should be quite hollow, as though they consisted of two layers.

To make a dough for the **Talos**, add a pinch of salt and very hot water to the maize flour, which you can also buy under the name corn meal or *polenta*. The mixture must be kneaded well with wet hands, on a surface sprinkled with a little wheat flour. Once the dough has been well kneaded it is set aside to rest for fifteen minutes and then divided into little balls, which are flattened with the hand to make small, thin cakes of about 3mm thick and 7cm across. These are placed, one by one, on a *talo burni*, a long-handled metal utensil used for cooking the *talos* over the fire. They are turned once and, when they are slightly brown, served alone, with milk or with a little creamy cheese, which can be put inside the *talos* to melt by cutting it open horizontally and then holding it over the fire once more. They are delicious, too, filled with bacon. *Talos* can also be made on top of the stove using a very large iron pan.

One evening, Nunchi and I sat around the fire, eating *talos* and chestnuts baked in a little earthenware pot, while she reminisced about growing up in the valley. Her childhood memories are happy ones, though there were few amusements and plenty of work. As a child she had milked the sheep and cows on her parents' small farm and later, during the Civil War, she went into service with a French family. She maintains that young people now do not know what real deprivation is, or realize how hard their parents worked at the same age, just to earn their keep. She recalls the apple trees in bloom, the chestnuts which are beginning to disappear and the paths which the shepherds would follow each year, up into the mountains. She particularly remembers the rare occasions when her mother would light the wood-fired oven and bake bread which filled the house with an irresistible aroma. What she would have given then to be able to eat her fill, although it was only maize bread!

In those days, nothing was allowed to go to waste in the kitchen. A number of these old dishes have survived. One, known as *Baztan-sopas*, is famous throughout the Basque Country. It belongs to the waste not, want not school of cookery. A sheep's head, intestines and tripe, together with a little of its fat, are used to make a broth, which is served over well-soaked sops of bread. Sometimes a little chilli is added to make the soup more spicy. The *sopa* is followed by a second course of the intestines, tripe and any pieces of meat from the head, chopped finely and fried in a pan with onion and olive oil. You could be forgiven for thinking that this dish sounds unappetizing, and, to be truthful, I have never been able to work up much enthusiasm for it, but its flavour and richness is greatly appreciated by the locals who consider its delicacy far superior to any other dishes made with mutton or lamb

Another interesting old delicacy is *Txuri-ta-Beltza* which is Basque for black and white. Again it comes from the days when nothing could be allowed to go to waste, but, if made properly, it can be quite delicious and it can still be found on restaurant menus in the valley.

 Txuri-Ta-Beltza is made from the large and small intestines of a lamb. Clean the small intestine, boil it and chop finely. Mix with garlic, an onion and a little parsley, all raw and finely chopped. This forcemeat is bound with 5 well beaten eggs. Then prepare the large intestine, clean it and turn it inside out like a glove. Fill with the stuffing, tie well and boil in water until it looks like a sausage and is thoroughly cooked. The second part of the recipe involves boiling the animal's blood. Once this is cooked put it in a casserole with a little oil, garlic and a small piece of fatty bacon. Sauté well and add a little tomato and onion sauce, prepared beforehand. Allow the sausage to cool and then cut into thin slices and serve with the blood cooked with tomato.

My own personal favourites among the shepherds' dishes are simpler *sopas* that the shepherds would cook in a three-legged iron pot over an open-air fire. One of them, *migas de pastor*, literally shepherds' breadcrumbs, is a dish made throughout Spain wherever man tends livestock in the hills. The only difference from one area to another is in the flavouring ingredients added to the bread; towards the south, for example, these include grapes. The speciality of the shepherds in the mountains of the north of Navarre, flavoured with ham and sausage, is quite delicious and very easy to make.

My father used to make a marvellous *migas de pastor*. He would cut the bread left over from the previous day into very thin pieces; these would be placed in a large serving dish and moistened by sprinkling a little warm water over them to which a pinch of salt had been added. Then he would melt a knob of lard in a frying-pan and fry three unpeeled cloves of garlic, cut in half. When they were golden brown he would remove them. The best part of the *migas* came next – the little pieces of cured ham and *chorizo* (spicy pork sausage) fried in the garlicky oil. Next the bread would be added and turned in the fat with a wooden spoon. Sometimes to make a more substantial dish, shepherds break some eggs into the bread in the frying-pan.

 A similar dish of which I am very fond, is called **Tostón de sopas de horno**, meaning oven-baked sops. For this a long loaf from the previous day is used and cut into small pieces. They are placed in a flameproof dish and water from cooking various green vegetables, such as .asparagus or cabbage, is poured over the top. Some cloves of garlic and a little cured ham cut into small cubes are fried in olive oil, a teaspoon of paprika added and mixed into the bread and the whole dish put into the oven until golden brown.

Bread dishes are primarily cooked during the winter months and *costrada* is one of the best examples. This recipe is a clever combination of fresh vegetables, *sopas de pan* (thinly cut bread), eggs and *chorizo*, which works to perfection. Although any kind of good quality *chorizo* could be added, the traditional *Pamplona chorizo* is ideal.

 This recipe for **Costrada** comes from my Navarrean grandmother. You need 300g (11oz) of bread, thinly cut and toasted in the oven, 150g (5oz) of *chorizo* cut very thin and slightly fried in a little olive oil, 2 onions and 5 carrots, both peeled, chopped, boiled in a little salt water until tender and puréed,

400 ml (14 fl oz) of vegetable stock, 2 eggs and salt. In an earthenware dish place one layer of bread, one of *chorizo* and one
of the vegetables. Repeat the layers until all the ingredients
have been used. Pour the stock over and place the dish in
a hot oven for about fifteen minutes. It is better if a little
liquid remains after cooking. Traditionally a few eggs were
broken open on top and then the dish was returned to the
oven for a few more minutes, but in my family the dish is
preferred without them.

By the beginning of this century, emigration had become common
practice. The young men would leave for California and Chile,
to work there as shepherds while they were still bachelors. Some
came back while they were still young, with a little money in
their knapsack, to marry a local girl. Many more returned late
in life, to retire to a comfortable house bought with the savings
they had accumulated during many years of effort and, usually,
loneliness and homesickness. Nunchi's eldest brother returned
from California some years ago and now lives alone in the mountains; he bakes *talos* and likes living in the silence which he became
accustomed to when he was in America. He worked in Idaho where
the first Basque shepherds arrived more than a century and a half
ago and there is still a Basque language television channel. Other
emigrants never came back. Today there are some three generations
of Basques in America keeping alive their customs, folklore and
the Basque language. Some, the cleverest among them, escape their
ten year work-contract and move to New York or Chicago, where
they eventually open a bar. Others set up restaurants in California.
In June every year the *chilenos*, literally the Chileans, the families
of those who emigrated to seek their fortune in South America,
come back to spend their holidays in the valley's hotels. The disappearance of the men left many unmarried women earlier this century, as a result, today there are many elderly spinsters. It also
helped to produce a tradition of late marriage. Nunchi, for example,
married Domingo when she was twenty-seven and that was considered relatively young since most men and women did not marry

until they were thirty. Now, most people marry slightly earlier as the doctor says that thirty is too old to start a family.

These days, there is hardly any Basque emigration to America and people can afford to set up a house at a much younger age. The economy of the valley is still based on the exploitation of its natural assets, such as timber, wool, coal, meat and cheese, but now they yield a good return. Tradition and modernity co-exist side by side. Elizondo, the capital of the district, is full of cars, banks and people living at an unheard of speed. Parents dream of sending the children to Pamplona or another university town, where they can be educated and be prepared for the world down beyond the mountains. Predictably, many of the *kaikus* Domingo makes are no longer used for their original purpose, but destined to rest on a shelf unit or in a glass case of a farmhouse in Elizondo. Nevertheless, small villages like Errazu, have clung on to many old traditions. Each village usually has its combined bar and shop, selling all sorts of food and gadgets and utensils for the house and the farm. At Arizcun a few kilometres from Errazu, the bar doubles as a restaurant and a music school, where the local *txistulary*, the man who plays the *txistu*, a regional wind instrument which has a very soft sound, teaches the children of the neighbourhood. The instruments used to play an important part in all the fiestas, as music and dance always do in the Basque Country, but unfortunately today few villages have kept their *txistularis*. In this sense, Arizcun is a fortunate village since it has retained everything that means most to its inhabitants: church, *pelota* court, restaurant and music. Old habits die hard here. Electricity and gas may have arrived, but the women still continue to go into mourning wearing black and covering their heads with a large black scarf.

Festivals remain a strong thread of continuity with the past. Christmas and Carnival (Shrove Tuesday) were the times when food was at its best in the past, with luxuries like wheat bread and honey or sugar sweetened desserts on the table. Many of these were milky puddings which made ingenious use of the abundance of dairy products. At Christmas, a *sopa cana*, a sweet almond milk found in many regions of Spain, is still traditionally eaten.

The ingredients for **Sopa cana** are, 3 litres (5 pints) of milk, 2 cinnamon sticks, 200 g (7 oz) of ground almonds, a tablespoonful of sugar, the fat from 2 chickens and the rind of half a lemon. Heat the milk with the cinnamon and when it comes to the boil add the almonds and lemon rind and simmer for a few minutes. In a separate pan melt the fat and then pour over the milk mixture and allow to thicken slightly. This is served with some pieces of buns called *suizos*, like currant buns. In some places the quantity of sugar is reduced, the bun omitted and the dish then served as a first course.

Nunchi also remembers, the village fiestas, those rare days when the air of the valley was full of happiness and the girls were dressed in the new frocks of flowered material, which they had spent months making. Many of the old festival traditions survive in the Baztan valley. The men dance the *mutil-dantzas* to the music of the *txistulary*. These folkdances remain a male preserve. In Errazu, encouraged by the spirit of change, the local girls have tried to dance the *mutil-dantzas*, but the men have set themselves firmly against this. Winds of change may well be abroad, but there are still some things which Basque men refuse to countenance.

In each season there are still reasons to celebrate. Often these are pagan rites, their ancient origins lost in time, fused with later religious customs in an attempt to sanctify them. At Christmas, for example, the coming of Jesus has become merged with the arrival of the Olentzero, an aged charcoal burner who comes down from the mountains on Christmas Eve, bringing great merriment and good cheer to the villagers. One of the local youths paints his face, dons a big hat, puts a pipe in his mouth and is then carried on a litter through the village by the other lads to the accompaniment of a series of folk songs in which they describe him as a drunkard and a glutton, as well as some more flattering terms. Carnival, at the beginning of Lent, similarly blends folklore and religion.

Among the Carnival celebrations the most famous takes place in the mountain village of Lanz. There a mysterious legendary person, known as Miel-Otxin, is paraded through the streets amongst the music and dancing of young people, some of them dressed up in large sacks. The unfortunate Miel always comes to rest in the bonfire. In Errazu and Arizcun, the young people also go round the farmhouses singing regional songs to the music of an accordion and asking for a contribution. At the first house they may be given a *txistorra*, at the next a basket of eggs or perhaps a chicken or some money. At every house there is something. Whatever they collect they then sell and on Shrove Tuesday they have a meal at one of the local restaurants. At the inn in Errazu, María Dolores, a cousin of Nunchi and Domingo, cooks the traditional Carnival dishes: pigs' trotters and *leche frita* or fried milk.

The pigs' trotters are halved, deboned, boiled and coated in flour and egg and fried in olive oil, then placed in an earthenware dish where they are cooked slowly on top of the stove with water or stock flavoured with onion browned in olive oil, one or two cloves of garlic and a sprig of parsley.

 The **Leche frita** is another milky dessert. For it you need 1 litre (1¾ pints) of milk, 250 g (9 oz) of sugar, 75 g (2½ oz) of cornflour, 7 egg yolks and 3 whole eggs, a tablespoonful of melted butter, a few drops of olive oil, a little flour, a cinnamon stick and some ground cinnamon. Put half the milk to boil with the cinnamon stick. Meanwhile dissolve the cornflour in the rest of the milk in a mixing dish. In a bowl beat the egg yolks and the whole eggs and pour over the milk and cornflour. Then add to the milk and cinnamon, stirring all the time; bring back to the boil and simmer a few minutes, then remove from the heat. Add the butter and pour the mixture into a shallow, rectangular dish or cake tin to cool. When cold, cut into small squares. Coat these with flour and egg and fry in olive oil until golden. Serve hot, sprinkled with ground cinnamon and icing sugar.

One of the oldest celebrations in the Basque Country is *La Mascarada Suletina*, the masquerade at Soule in the French Basque provinces where old invocations to bring good harvests are re-enacted. Five different characters take part in this dance, each one more extraordinary in appearance than the last: the *Txerrero*, sweeping away the evil spirits with his broom, the *Zamaltzain*, a horse, personifying the spirit of the maize; the *Edaridum* or inn-keeper's wife, a female figure symbolizing the cult of wine; the *Gatusain*, who dances with a kind of wooden trellis symbolizing the lightning which brings the rains needed by the crops and finally the *Ikurrindum* at the rear bearing a flag and representing the Nation.

Other feasts are linked to the strongly rooted local belief in witches. For while the Basques are not superstitious by nature – the philosopher, Miguel de Unamuno once described them as 'lacking in fantasy and creative imagination and, all in all, rather sceptical' – they believe strongly in ancient tribal traditions. The most famous example of this is the story of the witches of Zagarramurdi, a small village not far from Errazu and a few yards from the French frontier at Dancharinea. There is nothing particularly remarkable about the place; a church, two local restaurants, some twenty houses. Nearby, however, are a series of beautiful caves where a group of witches who are said to have terrorized the village held their sabbaths. Here on a plaque at the entrance to the caves, one can read their story: In the year 1610 a wave of witchcraft hysteria, of the sort which periodically gripped the Basque country, swept across the region; the inquisitor, Don Juan del Valle Alvarado, was sent to carry out an investigation. Forty men and women, said to be members of the witches sabbath, were arrested and taken away to Logroño, the capital of Rioja. The Inquisition accused these people of worshipping the Devil, practising metamorphosis, calling-up storms to shipwreck vessels making landfall or putting to sea at San Juan de Luz, putting curses on fields, animals and people, and of vampirism and necrophilism, among other things. As a result of all this twelve witches and wizards were burned at the stake, five of them in the form of an effigy, since they had already died in gaol, and the rest received punishments such as confiscation of their goods or incarceration for life.

Today all that remains are the caves, the Devil's cathedral, as they were afterwards known, and the stories of the vicissitudes of the people of Zagarramurdi with their witches. Amongst these legends is the tale of how the inhabitants of Zagarramurdi, in an effort to rid themselves of the witches, went in procession to the caves, one 15 August 1650. Once there the priest spread out a robe, which had been blessed and sprinkled with mustard seeds, to frighten away the witches for as many years as there were grains of mustard on the robe. None have been seen since.

Every year, in commemoration of that procession, a great banquet is held in the caves on the 15 August. This feast is the celebration of the *Zikiro*, the roasting of a castrated lamb by a very ancient method to symbolize the killing of the male witch. People from all parts of the Basque Country, even Bilbao, arrive between the 15 and the 19 August. Until just five or six years ago only men attended the banquet, but the women of the French Basque provinces decided that the time had come to break away from this long tradition and began to attend as well, swiftly followed, as one might expect, by the women from the other side of the border, who did not wish to be outdone. The great roast takes place in the main cave, in the middle of which they build a bonfire. Around its sides are wires supporting the stakes on which the joints are impaled vertically to roast. Each carcase is cut into four pieces. Apparently this is one of the best methods of roasting meat since the fat falls to the ground, rather than into the flames, and thus does not alter the flavour of the meat which cooks slowly and evenly; the fire cooks the meat both by convection and radiation. The lambs they roast have been raised on beans and local vegetables. One can eat as much as one wishes, followed by eggs cooked with peppers, finishing with a good meaty soup. Food, as always with the Basques, has become the excuse for all sorts of events.

The village inn, a fine building with its family coat of arms carved in stone over the main doorway, looks more like a farm than a restaurant. There are no bedrooms here, only meals twice a day, served in a large traditional dining-room on the first floor. An enormous front portico leads through to the cowsheds, the chicken coop and the pigsty. On the opposite side of the building, a wide wooden staircase leads up to the kitchen. Here María

Dolores, Nunchi's cousin, cooks excellent, if simple fare. Indeed, the inn has won such local fame that French cars can be found parked outside every day, their drivers lured by the homely dishes. Rumour has it that the beans cannot be bettered. 'Though the beans they cook in the town of Tolosa may be famous, they do not cast those of Errazu into the shade,' said María Dolores, her good nature shone through in an infectious smile. Then she explained how she prepares them. 'If they are freshly picked, they need no soaking. I put them into warm water to cook, but in the months of March and April I use cold water. A few drops of good olive oil, a small piece of salty, fatty bacon and a bit of cured ham, are all that are needed. If I happen to have any *txistorra* sausage, then I add that too. The beans must be boiled all morning, at first quite briskly, later on one side of the wood-burning stove.'

The kitchen of the inn is just the same as it must have been a century ago, and little different from that of the other farmhouses in the village. Traditionally, the kitchen is the focal point of daily life, the front room being used only when there are visitors. The floors are normally wooden and the walls covered with plaster painted a pastel colour. On the rear wall will be the low canopied fireplace and around it a number of stools where the family sit. Above the grate there would be iron bars on which to rest pots and pans.

Here, in the inn, neither gas nor solid fuel stoves have crossed the threshold: María Dolores cooks on the fine black iron range fuelled by wood. This type of stove is still widely used, even in some of the most prestigious restaurants, since the secret of some delicious Basque dishes consists merely of a drop of oil on the hotplate which separates fish or meat from the wooden fire. Probably one of the most memorable hake that I have ever eaten was cooked this way. The expert cook simply basted the thick slice of fish sizzling on the hotplate with a little of the best quality olive oil from time to time. After seven or eight minutes she turned it over with kitchen tongs, and then deftly removed the backbone and let it cook a little longer. The taste was unique.

The inn's dining-room is furnished simply with wooden tables and an open iron hearth, which is lit when diners arrive; in winter, when the valley is very cold, there is nothing like a wood fire and a drop of Navarrese red wine to raise the spirits.

In María Dolores' restaurant there is no written menu. The dishes simply change with the seasons and their festivals, following local ingredients and those which can be bought in Elizondo, in fact most of the dishes at the inn are based on the meat of the bullocks which graze every day on the excellent pastures of the valley, and produce meat of a quality which is hard to find elsewhere in the Peninsula. One of the inn's specialities is *redondo de carne*, rolled beef, which María Dolores cooks with onion, garlic, parsley, carrot, white wine and a drop of wine vinegar. The best cut for this is skirt, which is reasonably priced, with the meat prepared and tied in a roll. Both the meat and the vegetables are sautéed in a little oil, then the wine is added, followed by a little good meat or vege-table stock and the dish is left to cook slowly until the meat is tender and succulent. There are endless variations on this recipe; at home we prepare it with a forcemeat of boiled ham and some very thin omelette, to which slices of olive have been added which give the dish a lovely flavour.

In the autumn when pigeon fly from northern Europe and enter the natural passes through the Pyrenees in search of fine weather, pigeon dishes feature on the menus of the valley restaurants and inns. Some birds meet their deaths in one of these passes between Echalar and Sare. Many nets are stretched between the trees whose tops form a natural pathway and the men of Echalar await, posit-ioned in high wooden watchtowers on the slopes of the valley. Should the pigeon be flying very high then these men will hoist into the air a series of white paddles, rather like rackets, which the pigeon, flying overhead, take to be sparrow-hawks since these usually attack from below. In fear they swoop down steeply, seek-ing out the protection of the slopes amongst the paths through the trees. Many are trapped in the nets, others are brought down by the shots of hunters who have converged from all over the Basque Country. The number of birds killed in this way is small, but the dramatic spectacle of the flocks flying into the nets, against the backdrop of the Pyrennean passes, attracts tourists to come here for the weekend to watch. Here are two excellent local recipes for pigeon.

 To make **Braised pigeon** first the birds are plucked, dressed and cleaned thoroughly, then, in an earthenware casscrole they are browned in a little good olive oil and set aside. One or two peeled and quartered apples, a little finely chopped onion, one or two carrots and a leek are also sautéed until golden. Then the pigeon are returned to the dish, together with a little chopped parsley, a small glass of Navarrese white wine, and, once more, a little stock. The dish is cooked on a low heat until the birds are tender, when they are removed from the casserole and the sauce is strained. Traditionally they were served by putting some slices of fried-bread in the bottom of the dish beneath each pigeon, and sauce poured over them. The dish is then returned to the heat and served when it is nice and hot.

 Most recently wood pigeon has been used for variations on this interesting dish. Juan José Castillo, one of the fathers of Basque cookery, today prepares a delicious **Pigeon in sauce**. Each pigeon which has been plucked and cleaned, is cut into quarters, boned and covered with a cloth, while the rest of the dish is prepared: Sautée in a frying-pan 2 cloves of garlic, 2 carrots and 1 onion, all finely chopped, in a little olive oil. When they are golden brown add some poultry stock, prepared in advance and a little thyme. Simmer for a few minutes and then add the pigeons' liver which has been brought to the boil and crushed to a paste with a pestle and mortar, or a fork. Stir a little until the liver mixture thickens the sauce and then remove from the heat. The pigeon are then arranged on the plates and flambéed with a little brandy from Jerez or Catalonia. Meanwhile, the sauce should be warmed again before pouring over the meat. This should be served immediately, accompanied by small new potatoes and a green vegetable, stir-fried with oil and garlic and served on a separate plate.

As one might expect, lamb is widely available in the mountains between December and May; the best kind is *lechal* or milk-fed, spring lamb. María Dolores thinks that the best way of cooking this is to roast it in the oven of a wood-fired stove, sprinkled with salt and with a few rashers of bacon laid over it. A little garlic can also be added, but not too much. But the best known dish from these parts is, *cordero al chilindrón*, lamb cooked with peppers. This method of cooking lamb is common to a wide area in the north-east of the Peninsula.

 For **Cordero al chilindrón** you need a leg of lamb, deboned, 4 dried red peppers, an onion, a small glass of white wine, a little meat stock, garlic and salt. Cut the meat into chunks and brown it in olive oil in a frying-pan. Transfer to a traditional earthenware casserole. In the remaining oil, sauté the onion and garlic and once they are golden brown add the meat, draining off the oil. Then add the wine, cook for a few minutes over quite a hot flame, reduce the heat before putting in the peppers, cut into strips, add a little tomato sauce, which has been prepared in advance. Cook for a few minutes before adding stock to cover. It should be cooked slowly until all the ingredients are tender and ready to serve. This sort of dish is often even better the following day. My grandmother, who used to make excellent *chilindrón*, would sometimes add small pieces of potato and some raw tomato.

Not all the food of the valley is traditional, some small restaurants and local hotels catering largely for visitors have introduced dishes which are strictly modern in their inspiration, but the people of the valley rarely go to such restaurants. They have neither the time nor the inclination to do so.

At the small hotel near Errazu a van arrives every morning from San Sebastián loaded with all kinds of fish and shellfish as well as any other ingredients which the cook needs, but which it would otherwise be impossible to obtain in the area. Nonetheless, the chef still also uses the best of regional produce, as in this warm salad of brains and shellfish, a combination of raw vegetables, meat and seafood.

To prepare this **Ensalada templada de sesos y mariscos** you need the brains of 2 milk-fed lambs, 300 g (13 oz) of shellfish – prawns, scampi, etc., a few leaves of lettuce, batavia, endive and watercress, a little carrot, some mayonnaise and whole grain mustard, a little parsley, olive or peanut oil, wine vinegar, a little butter, ½ a clove of garlic, a few drops of lemon juice and a pinch of salt. Turn out the well-cleaned brains into a pan of water containing a little vinegar, and cook for a few minutes. Once they are done remove from the water and cool. Next prepare the salad ingredients, clean them, cut them up and arrange on the plates, dressing them with a light dressing made with olive or peanut oil and a little wine vinegar. Then sauté the shellfish lightly with a few drops of oil, lemon juice and if you wish, a little garlic, which can be sprinkled over the salads afterwards. Similarly sauté the brains with a little butter, having first cut them into slices. Arrange them on the salads interspersed between the pieces of shellfish. The finishing touches are a little sauce made from mayonnaise and mustard, julienne-carrot and some sprigs of parsley.

The chef has also adapted the traditional recipe for *talos* with cheese, according to the principles of the new style cooking, to make delicious croquettes.

 To prepare twenty **Croquetas de queso** you need 1½ litres of milk (2½ pints), 50 g (2 oz) of butter, 50 g (2 oz) of flour, 150 g (5 oz) of creamy cheese, salt, pepper and ground nutmeg and for the batter 200 g (7 oz) of flour, 50 ml (2 fl oz) of oil, 1 small glass of water, 3 egg whites and a teaspoon of baking powder. Make a roux with the butter and flour, add the milk to make a sauce, add a little salt, pepper and nutmeg. Add the cheese, blend well and allow the mixture to cool. Form small balls of about 2.5 cm diameter. To prepare the batter mix in a bowl the flour, oil, water, baking powder and salt. Mix well to form a smooth paste, adding a little water, and cover with a cloth. Set aside for about twenty minutes or until the mixture has doubled in volume. Beat the egg whites until stiff and fold into the smooth paste. Dip each ball into the batter and fry in very hot oil.

It is Saturday and the Echandis, their sons and grandchildren have congregated around the dining-table. The contrast between the old villagers from Errazu and the children from Pamplona is interesting, the distance between them being much greater than merely that of the generation gap. The children will never learn to play the *txistu* or dance the *mutil-danzas* properly, although they still eat roast chestnuts and *talos* most weekends. They can feel the spell of the valley, Canela's barking and the walks through the birches with their grandfather, but tomorrow they will be back in the city again, speaking Castilian and with the *kaiku* far away from their thoughts.

Over the last few years Domingo has tried to teach several youngsters his trade, but they soon tired and preferred to go off to the town to make their fortune; *kaikus* involve too much work and little economic gain. This saddens Domingo as he feels that his cherished *kaiku* will disappear once these ones are worn away, sadly with time and not use.

THE CIDER AND
WINE HOUSES

Over the centuries, Basque men, sociable by nature, have searched out places where they can eat and drink and meet their friends. A number of those who have written on the subject believe that it was probably in quayside taverns that the men first gathered, and that the cider houses inland and the fishermen's guilds, which exist in every port, grew up later. We do not know the exact origins of the first *sidrerías*, where cider has been made and sold since at least medieval times, but it is not hard to imagine how they were born in the inland hamlets of Guipúzcoa, where almost every *caserío*, or farmstead, has a cider-mill, to supply the family's needs. When the apple harvests were plentiful and the *caseríos* made more than they needed, the surplus would be offered to friends and neighbours at a moderate price, or bartered in exchange for eggs or fodder. Probably one farmer, a keen cider-maker who produced a surplus every year, decided that the *kupelas*, or vat, should be tasted before the cider had completely finished fermenting in April. Naturally he wanted to share such an exciting moment with his neighbours who bought his cider, so he would have invited them over for the tasting. As was customary, they would have brought food: one lamb cutlets, another cheese and walnuts, a third a *cazuela* or casserole of cod. Thus the *probateko*, or tasting of the cider before it is totally fermented, was born.

From here it was a short step to the farmer's wife's business plans, deciding that they should sell the new cider for drinking before it was bottled. It goes almost without saying that some food would have been served at the same time. She would have prepared simple, rustic dishes using seasonal ingredients from the farm. The men from the hamlet and perhaps further afield in the valley, began to gather here to drink and eat, to talk and play cards, and so the *sidrerías* evolved. Needless to say, the women, as always with such activities, were excluded.

The *sidrerías* became an important focus for social life in the green valleys and hills of the rural areas. Simultaneously, cider-making grew in importance and it became closely regulated by the *fueros*, or local laws. We know, for example, that in 1556 in the city of Tolosa, instructions for cider producers were laid down by the Town Council and read out to local congregations during mass. The sale of cider was also controlled. Before the season began, the farmer-producers would congregate at the Town Hall, the vats having all been numbered, and lots would be drawn under strict supervision for the order in which the vats could be broached. During the season, the local town-crier would proclaim the broaching of each vat for sale, announcing the name of the farm and the date the cider was to go on sale.

With the improvement of the roads in the seventeenth century, cider began to be ousted by the wines of Alava and particularly Navarre and, despite protection by the *fueros*, to lose some of its monopoly in the countryside. By the end of the eighteenth century, the *sidrerías* had almost entirely moved to the coastal areas and were frequented by sailors and traders. Now cod omelettes and grilled sardines usually constituted the accompanying menu.

Nonetheless cider-drinking remained widespread throughout the Basque Country, and with nineteenth-century industrialization, the habit reached the growing and developing towns. However, the city cider houses, such as those of San Sebastián, were not set up in detached houses, but in the basements of blocks of flats, where they were reached by steep staircases. Though their location had changed, the same details persisted: the great vats, the canopied open fireplace for grilling sardines, the long trestle tables and benches. There was no electricity. All that was needed was the light of a candle or oil lamp.

But with the shift to so-called prosperity wine, then considered a more sophisticated drink, the *sidrerías* slowly declined until, by the 1930s, practically all of them had closed. As a result, many of the apple orchards with ancient indigenous varieties were lost and cereals were planted in their place. Today, however, when the Basques are reverting to many traditions close to their hearts, the *sidrerías* are becoming fashionable again and cider-tasting, *probateko*, which used to be enjoyed only by a select few invited by the owner, has become an entertainment open to all, even women. During the season the cider houses are bursting at the seams, but, as in the past, they remain unique to the province of Guipúzcoa. More than half are to be found in the city of San Sebastián and the rest are in small nearby towns like Hernani, Lasarte, Urnieta, Usurbil, Oyarzun, and Asteasu.

The beloved old apple trees are blooming anew as more real cider is made every year. A replanting programme is slowly beginning to meet some of the hugely increased demand for local varieties like Arrezila, Reineta, Txalaka, Bizkai-sagarra and Aldako-sagarro which make the best cider. Acidic apples result in paler, soft in the palate, almost transparent and slightly *pétillant* ciders, while bitter apples give a deeper colour, but not such a dry finish. Today, manufacture is highly controlled and the *sidrerías* engage an expert under contract to oversee every detail and to ensure quality control at every stage. The laws governing cider-making have also changed. Thin, unfermented cider is not allowed in many places but the vats may be broached for sale whenever their owners choose. In other respects, cider-making has changed little over the centuries; the same types of barrels and buildings are used. In the autumn the different varieties of apple are picked. Apparently the first apples to fall from the tree are usually worm-eaten and should be discarded since they would impart an unpleasant taste.

At Celaya's, a typical *sidrería* in the locality of Astigarraga, a few kilometres from San Sebastián and very near the village of Hernani, the cider-making starts in autumn. At present half the apples they use are produced in other regions of Spain, but the ones which truly give character to Celaya's cider are selected from the *caserío* of a very old friend. It is hoped that within four years the total requirement will be Basque.

When the apples Celaya has bought arrive at the cider house, he and his friends quickly sort through them, throwing out any which are damaged. First the fruit passes between two rotating drums, which crush them without damaging the pips, since this would give a bitter flavour. The apple pulp, *patxa*, emerges from the crusher, then goes into the *tolare* or press, where it macerates for about twenty-four hours. The apples are then pressed very gently some eight times, until all the juice has dripped through the fine mesh of the press. Next it is transferred to the vats, which in the case of the Celaya's cider house, contain seven, eleven and twenty-five thousand litres. After a few hours the first tumultuous fermentation takes place spontaneously, later giving way to a second, much gentler and more gradual fermentation, with a cap of foam, the *txapela*, forming on the top. The fermentation and clarification processes last about three months, although the secondary fermentation remains active longer than this. Great still-ness and a constant temperature of between seven and fourteen degrees are necessary if the cider is to be good. The result is a light cider of about five per cent alcohol. In January, the cider is ready for tasting although it has not yet completely finished fermenting. By May it will be ready and some 300,000 bottles will be filled. It is neither racked nor filtered and bottling is gravity-fed so that the natural sparkle is not lost. Some will go to gastro-nomic societies who bought a particular *kupela* at the beginning of the year, the remainder to faithful private customers.

During the intervening months, Celaya opens his doors to sell the new cider, just as the *sidrerías* did of old, and hangs a branch over the door to signify that the cider is ready for tasting. The only difference is that now it is so difficult to find a table, that you have to reserve in advance. Nevertheless, despite its new-found popularity, this remains a largely male preserve. On my first visit with two other women, a hush fell and all eyes turned towards us as we walked through the door. But it would be wrong to imagine that this is a haven where men come so that they can talk and drink as they please without their wives' friends telling tales. Rather, you sense in the atmosphere the inherent Basque sense of male solidarity, in sharing food, wine and talk with other men friends.

The main room of the *sidrería* is enormous, almost barn-like, with rows of wooden trestle tables covered with red and white checked cloths. There are no chairs. Everyone stands in groups, eating and talking enthusiastically. On the tables lie forks, baskets of bread, toothpicks and salt cellars. A waiter brings new arrivals thin, clear glass-tumblers.

During the evening people move back and forth between this and another large room, a huge hall where twenty or more wooden vats or *kupelas*, raised above the ground on large concrete plinths, line the walls. The man in charge of the cider pronounces the word *mojón*, which means that he is about to remove the *txiri*, a small wooden stick which seals a minute hole in the vat. The tasters line up and take it in turn to intercept the flow of the thin stream of cider gushing out, holding their glasses at an angle to it so that the cider hits the glass, splashing and foaming, but without any spilling on to the floor. When the foreman decides that enough cider has been drawn from a vat he re-inserts the stick in the hole and moves on to the next one. During the three-hour session, all the vats in the cellar will be opened and tasted. Quite a small quantity is drawn off each time and one has to drink each glass almost in one gulp in the ensuing seconds, otherwise the cider loses its loveliness and attractive sparkle. When the taster goes back to his table it is with an empty glass. Then he waits a while, talks to his neighbour, eats and, when he feels like it, returns to taste the contents of another vat. It goes without saying that first attempts at taking cider from the vat without spilling it are invariably laughable, but after making three or four trips you soon become quite an expert. Anyway, the worst that can befall you is that the stream of cider will hit your hand rather than the glass, or that some will be wasted; this tends to be frowned upon by the older customers, who rarely spill a single drop.

The food at Celaya's could not be more simple: meat, fish or *cazuelas* that you bring with you for grilling or reheating; cod and onion, or cod, onion and green pepper omelettes, cheese and *membrillo*, quince paste and walnuts, to finish. When customers arrive, Celaya takes their orders and carries away any food they have brought with them. Soon it is in the hands of the grill cook, who stands under an enormous canopy over a metal grid and hot coals. Occasionally he adds chopped garlic and a little olive oil to the mutton, lamb and *chuletón*, rib of beef, the sardines and, a particular favourite, grilled bream. Smoke billows out perfuming the air with a woody scent of sea and land.

 To prepare **Besugo a la brasa**, sea bream cooked on embers, the fish must be cleaned well and the scales removed. Then it is sprinkled with a little salt. It can either be grilled whole or split open so that it cooks more quickly. If it is cooked whole, once it is ready, it is split open, the backbone is removed and a little olive oil in which some garlic slices have been fried is drizzled over it. Some cooks like to add a little chilli to the warm oil, others sprinkle the fish with a few drops of cider-vinegar before serving.

In the kitchen proper, two expert cooks cope with the endless demand for omelettes. Earthenware casseroles stand warming to the side of the fierce heat from the coal-fuelled range. Large wicker baskets hold mounds of green peppers, onion and fresh farmhouse bread. The cooks work fast and furiously, dividing their attention between the fire, the chopping board and the eggs themselves, which are first beaten, then poured into heavy frying pans made of cast iron. I have never eaten such good omelettes as those found in and around San Sebastián.

To prepare a **Tortilla de cebolla y bacalao**, salt-cod, parsley and onion omelette for two people you need 4 eggs, 250 g (9 oz) of desalinated cod, 2 medium-sized onions, 2 tablespoons of chopped parsley, olive oil and salt. Put a little oil in a casserole with the onion, chopped, leave to sweat very slowly until the onion is golden brown, then remove from the heat. Put a frying-pan on the heat and transfer the contents of the casserole, including the oil, into it. Then add the flaked cod and the parsley and leave to cook for a few minutes, stirring to prevent it from sticking. Finally, add the beaten eggs. The omelette is turned over by means of a plate or folded in half; but in either case, it should still be slightly runny in the middle.

Although there is little choice in the dishes prepared at the *sidrería* you will not leave without having sampled half a dozen dishes on top of your own. On my visit to Celaya's, when we were sharing our table with four students, I found myself trying first our neighbours' spring lamb; a delicious dish of dried peppers with garlic and olive oil and several *cazuelas de pescado*, fish stews. Those and many other dishes that you can see on every table have been cooked beforehand and brought in to be heated up. One dish that I tasted in this way, a *Bacalao a la vizcaina*, was a truly memorable experience.

 To prepare **Salt-cod with vizcaina sauce** you need 1 kg (2 lbs) of dried cod, cut into large squares and desalinated, 100 ml (3½ fl oz) of olive oil, 2 large onions, chopped, a little lard, 100 g (3½ oz) of cured ham, parsley, 5 dried *choricero* peppers, 2 boiled egg yolks dissolved in a little water. Place the fish in a large saucepan with plenty of cold water and heat very slowly for about forty-five to sixty minutes at a very low temperature, otherwise the quality will deteriorate rapidly. To prepare the *Vizcaina sauce*, place the olive oil, a little ham and pork belly, together with the onion and parsley in a dish and cook very slowly for about two hours to avoid the onion caramelizing. Add a little water and cook for a further hour. Set aside and sieve the sauce, adding the dried peppers, which have been soaking for a few hours in cold water. Then add the egg yolks. Place the pieces of fish in a large earthenware dish, making certain that the skins are on top. Pour over the sauce, and heat very slowly for a few minutes more.

Another recipe, **Cazuela de merluza a la sidra**, is also very typical of the *sidrerías*. To prepare this fresh hake with cider you need for six people 6 hake steaks, each weighing about 350 g (12 oz), 3 shallots, 1 clove of garlic, 1 green pepper, 6 tablespoons of dry cider, 200 ml (7 fl oz) olive oil, 1 tablespoon of chopped parsley, a little chilli powder and a pinch of salt. Put the oil in a large casserole and heat. When it is quite hot add the garlic, shallots and green pepper, all chopped. Fry until soft then remove from the heat for the oil to cool a little. At this point, put the hake carefully into the casserole and return to the heat. At this stage the dish should be gently rocked from side to side continuously for several minutes. While still following this procedure, add the cider and then cover the casserole. Cook slowly for fifteen minutes. Add a little chilli and immediately before serving, the chopped parsley.

Nueva cocina vasca, or the new style of cooking, also incorporates cider in various dishes, among them monkfish cooked with the white parts of chard and cider.

 To prepare **Rape con sidra y vainas** you need 1 monkfish weighing about 750 g (1½ lbs), 2 finely chopped shallots, 100 ml (3½ fl oz) of cider, 1 tablespoon of hollandaise sauce, 100 g (3½ oz) of chard stalks, chopped, and 100 ml (3½ fl oz) of fresh cream. In a saucepan boil some salted water and cook the chard until tender. Clean the fish well and remove the backbone. Put 750 ml (1¼ pints) of water, the cider and the fishbones into a saucepan and cook for about ten minutes. Strain the stock into a large pan and then put the filleted monkfish into it and poach for several minutes. Transfer the fish to hot plates for serving. To make the sauce, sauté the shallots or baby onions in a little butter, add ½ a glass of the fish stock and the cream. Reduce until the sauce thickens a little then remove from the heat and add the holandaise sauce. Arrange the chard on top of the fish fillets and pour over the sauce. The dish should be served immediately.

Today the cider houses are here to stay. Every day they are more popular with young people who may not be prepared to cook as many extra dishes as other customers, but who enjoy the easy ambience of these places in winter, and the prices, which as long as you are prepared to go easy on the food, are still affordable. Many of the different groups meet in the same place every week throughout the season until May, when the cider-maker takes the branch down from the doorway to signify that he has done his work and that the *sidrería* will be closed until the following January.

——

Guetaria is a small fishing town in Gúipuzcoa province. Early in the morning on clear days, a great sea mist forms and settles over the hill-tops only a few kilometres inland, but on the slopes close to the sea, tall vines look to the sun to gild their leaves; for while the town makes its living from the sea its pleasure is derived from wine. This is where *txakolí* is made. A cheerful, slightly acidic wine, *txakolí* may be red or white, though providing that they have been well made, the best are the youthful and *pétillant* whites.

We know little about the history of wine on the Cantabrian slopes. It was the Romans who promoted viticulture to the area and later, in medieval times, the Pilgrim Route to Santiago which gave rise to the planting of vines. In the sixteenth century the excellence of the wines was recognized and those from Guetaria, in particular, were renowned for the high quality. The grape variety was, and still is, Hondarribi Zuri, or white, which occupies more than eighty per cent of the vineyard and the black, or Beltza, continues to be used to soften the rather acid wine produced from the former. In his book *The Wines of Spain*, Jan Read states that the Zuri is similar to the Courbu of the Jurancon area of France. Other writers maintain that the Belza belongs to the Bordeaux Cabernet Franc family.

Until the eighteenth century, *txakolí* was protected from nearby competition by the local *fueros* or privileges, but when they were abolished by the General Juntas of Guipúzcoa in 1830, decline set in. The market became dominated by wines from other areas, mainly the Rioja and Navarre, where the climate was less capricious and thus the crop practically guaranteed. The crisis was precipitated by several other factors too. Industrialization led to preoccupation with financial viability and the poor, romantic Cantabrian vineyards knew nothing of such things. Moreover, the great vine plagues, oidium, mildew and above all, phylloxera, which were to eradicate the wine-map of almost all of Europe, would prove a devastating blow. Of the 2,500 acres of the Basque Country planted with vines in 1800 fewer than eight hundred remained by the end of the nineteenth century. At present *txakolí* vineyards are limited to only 120 acres along the coast, in Guetaria and Zarauz, both in the province of Guipúzcoa, and Baquio and Balmaseda, in Vizcaya. At least these vines have survived and can look optimistically to the future. Recently, a new denomination of origin, *Txakolí de Guetaria*, was created and dedicated men have given their lives and money to the hard task of making unprecedented wines of high standards

Pedro Chueca, who lives in a beautiful old house next to the village church, is one of the men to whom Guetaria owes this new denomination. A small thin man with a gentle face and generous spirit, his love for his vineyard and devotion to wine-making, make themselves felt instantly. His grandfather Silvestre was the first in the family to plant vines on a high hillside which falls precipitously to the sea. His work involved an intense struggle against nature, so wild and luxuriant there. In fact the site was only one of the problems: this is an area whose rainfall is one of the highest in Europe. However, the microclimate of the vinegrowing slopes of Guetaria favoured Silvestre. It never froze, the average temperature was relatively high and the slopes faced south-east, thus achieving the best possible exposure to the sea-breezes which dry off the leaves and grapes. In spite of all the great problems, the vines produced bunches of grapes which yielded a golden juice.

Pedro inherited the vineyards from his mother, Silvestre's daughter. His uncle Fernando, a family benefactor, sent him to the French School at San Sebastián where he learned French before Castilian. Later, he was to spend four months in the Champagne region, in the home of Raymond a wine-maker, where he learned the basics of viticulture and vinification. Since then much has changed. When Pedro started, the small wooden wine barrels would arrive by ox-cart and one never knew whether they would arrive at all, or what state they might be in. Now bottles bearing the name Txomin Echániz, the brand under which the Chueca family's wine is marketed, are distributed by great lorries which leave the new winery every day for all parts of Spain.

Although Pedro is now retired, he spends every day in the vineyard. 'My two boys' hands are not enough by themselves', he explains. In winter, when the vinestock rests and has no sap in its veins, pruning is one of the most time-consuming tasks. As the cold season progresses they spread a little fertilizer on the land so that when the time comes, they will give better results. In spring life returns and the sap rises once more. This is Pedro's favourite season: the first buds appear, followed by the first leaves, and little by little the canopy of foliage thickens. Blossoming occurs in May and, after self-fertilization, the tiny fruits which will hang below the foliage appear under the daily scrutiny of the Chuecas. Summer progresses. This is when the vineyard needs sun and Pedro examines the sea and sky, reading into the clouds and winds to interpret what good or ill each portends. If the vines receive all the sun they need, they will produce a sufficient sugar level in the grapes so that the wine will not seem too acidic, or the alcohol content too low. In October extra hands are taken on for the grape harvest, the year's most important task. These will be the longest most worrying days of all, but also the happiest. At the end of each day's work the air is full of the scent of wine and of grilled fresh fish.

Prior to the construction of a new winery, right in the vineyard, the production took place in the cellar of the house, near the port. Today *txakolí* production is much easier. This is because Pedro achieved his dream, a new winery, thanks to the efforts of his sons. On the first floor live the younger Chuecas, the family of one of Pedro's sons. On the ground floor there is a production plant and a cellar where the vats, which until recently were the only vessels used for fermentation and storage, share their place with the new technology which has considerably improved the quality of this delicate wine.

It is only a matter of minutes from the moment when the grape is picked to its arrival, via tractor and trailer, at the winery. There the fruit is tipped into a chute hidden at the entrance to the building. Without being crushed the grapes are fed into a horizontal press and, in order to achieve a high quality result, the must is drawn off into large temperature-controlled stainless steel tanks. A small quantity is still fermented in wooden barrels, just as it has been since time immemorial. Normally the wine is neither filtered nor racked, but kept on the lees, the idea being to retain the natural carbon-dioxide content which helps preserve it and gives it life. Although one of the great problems faced by *txakolí* has always been the low alcohol content – generally barely the ten per cent traditionally attained by naturally effervescent wines – the addition of sugar to the must is forbidden by Spanish law but here the Chuecas are lucky. The wines made in the Guetaria area have always exceeded ten and a half per cent, rising even to eleven per cent in some years.

Txakolí is bottled in April, when the secondary malolactic fermentation is almost complete. However, before this happens the contents of each *kupelak*, vat, will be tasted, not only by its owners but also by their direct customers: the chefs and the various gastronomic societies who travel around the *bodegas*, vineyards, and farms to buy the year's best wine.

The tasting room is spacious and adorned by antique wooden chests, metal artefacts and several pictures, among them one large composition, presented to Pedro by an artist-friend which depicts the *txakolí* landscape. In the upper part of the painting a luxuriant climbing vine grows on a trellis so thick that the light cannot penetrate its foliage. The leaves are unnaturally dark, of olive and brown shade, the bunches of grapes are all golden yellow, almost glaring. Below the vine and trellis there is the surface of a sea in which two fish swim, one an intense red, the other, blue. Sea and woodland, foam and bubbles, apparently float together down a river.

Here, in the tasting room, the men who have come to buy will congregate. In contrast to the cider house, the buying of *txakolí* and the *probateko* is still the exclusive domain of the male. At the Chuecas's vineyard the introduction of new technology and quality standardization mean that the *probateko* has lost much of its meaning, but it remains in the *bodegas* of other, more traditional winemakers where little has changed over the years.

In the old days Pedro used to invite his friends to eat after the tasting. He still has vivid memories of the endless nights spent sitting along wooden benches on either side of the old oak table, enjoying the dishes prepared in the kitchen above by his wife, often using their own wine in the dish as she would for *dorada a la marinera*, gilthead seaman's style. This fish is rather insipid and this recipe suits it very well.

 To prepare the **Dorada a la marinera** you need a fish weighing 1kg (2 lbs), very fresh with its scales removed and thoroughly cleaned, 1 chopped onion, 1 clove of garlic, 2 large tomatoes, a little sweet paprika, parsley, a tablespoon of flour, pepper, a glass of *txakolí* and a pinch of salt. Place the gilthead in a pan of cold water and poach until cooked. Drain it well and transfer to a serving dish. Put a little olive oil into an earthenware casserole and in it fry the onion, garlic, tomato, parsley and the paprika. When it is almost half cooked, add the wine and reduce by half. Stir in the flour which has been mixed with a little of the liquid from poaching the fish and cook on a moderate heat for twenty minutes. Strain and pour the sauce over the fish on a serving dish.

Pedro's favourite dishes are always the simplest ones. If he is at home one of the things he likes best is a good plate of potatoes cooked with wine, which his wife often prepares. Although this recipe usually calls for some sort of pork sausage which Pedro describes as *calceta*, a thick woollen stocking, Milagro's version could not be simpler and more tasty.

 For **Patatas al txakolí** you need for four people 1kg (2 lbs) of potatoes, 2 dried red peppers, 1 clove of garlic, olive oil and a generous dash of wine to give it flavour. First the red peppers must soak in water for a couple of hours and then be cut up into strips. Peel the potatoes and cut them into two or four pieces. Pour a little olive oil into an earthenware casserole and fry a clove of garlic until golden; then remove it from the oil and add to the potatoes to sauté until slightly browned. At this stage add the wine and then the strips of pepper, together with ½ a clove of garlic, peeled and very finely chopped. Add water to cover the potatoes and bring to the boil, then reduce the heat so that they cook slowly. Sometimes eggs are added to poach for about five minutes before serving the potatoes.

Pedro's wife also makes an excellent dish of bass with *txakolí* and potatoes, which is her son Inaki's favourite.

 To prepare **Lubina con patatas al txakolí** for six people you need a fish of about 2 kg (4 lbs) weight, ½ kg (1 lb) of potatoes cut into thin rounds, 2 glasses of txacoli and some slices of lemon to insert into small incisions which are made in the fish. Place the potatoes in an oven dish and pour over a few drops of olive oil. Then put the bass on top and place the dish in a moderate oven 200°C (400°F, Gas mark 6). After fifteen minutes take it out and baste with the juices before putting it back for another fifteen minutes – the moment when the wine should be added. It will need another ten to fifteen minutes to be ready and slightly underdone.

Although *txakolí* has always been drunk in a more private way, in the province of Vizcaya the wine is associated with the *caserío-txakolí*, which fulfil the same role as Guipúzcoa's cider houses. However, in contrast to the cider house the *caserío-txakolí* has gradually lost its importance and may well soon disappear. Not so long ago, when they flourished, there were *txakolí*-roads through Vizcaya. A branch of bay-tree fixed to various trees along the road indicated the route to take. If its leaves were fresh something delicious was waiting at the journey's end; if, on the other hand, they were withered, it was probably wiser to come back the following year.

It was in these *caseríos-txakolí*, where it was difficult to obtain fresh fish, that cooking with *bacalao* really flourished. Every day hundreds of dishes of *bacalao al pil-pil, a la vizcaina* or simply with green peppers and potatoes or onions would be made. Another fine recipe, *bacalao Club-Ranero*, created by the French chef Caverivière as a farewell gesture to the Club in Vizcaya where he had worked, also became part of the repertoire of great Basque cod specialities found in places where *txakolí* is served.

The dish that follows is simply a version of *bacalao al pil-pil*, that is to say, salt-cod cooked with olive oil and garlic, to which is added a sautéed mixture of onion, tomatoes, green peppers and dried red peppers, together with the thickened sauce, an emulsion of oil and garlic, in which the slices of cod were first cooked.

 For the **Sautéed mixture for this bacalao** you need ½ kg (1lb) of fresh tomatoes, peeled and chopped, ½ kg (1lb) of onions, also peeled and chopped, 2 green peppers, deseeded and diced, 2 large chopped cloves of garlic, the flesh of 4 dried red peppers, soaked in advance for three to four hours, a little fresh parsley and some olive oil. Pour the oil into an earthenware casserole and sautée the onion until it softens a little, then add the tomato, garlic and green pepper. Cook gently, taking care that the pieces do not disintegrate. Then add the soaked dried pepper and a little chopped parsley. Transfer the fried mixture to another casserole and place the slices of cod on top of it, leaving the oil and garlic behind. This is when the emulsion sauce is made by beating the oil and garlic quite hard by moving the frying-pan until a perfect emulsion is achieved, thus changing the colour of the sauce. It should be almost white and the oil completely absorbed. Then add this sauce to the fish casserole, cook a little more and it is ready.

Today with the *caseríos-txakolí* disappearing, the restaurants and *asadores* or grill houses, found around Guetaria are taking their place as somewhere to relax, eat and drink well in the countryside. Families often travel here, particularly in summer, to sample the local *txakolí* and fish. Sometimes, when they have family visitors, the Chuecas too, go down to one of the *asadores*. As many as ten, twelve or more of them, including the grandchildren, sit down to eat under one of the canopies erected outside the establishment.

Most of the *asadores* in Guetaria are to be found in the harbour area. The grill proper, an iron construction on four legs which usually has wheels, is placed near the main entrance to the bar or restaurant to which it belongs and consists of a large metal grid resting on a sort of cart about a metre and a half long, which contains burning coals. The grid is usually divided into two sections which are used for cooking meat and fish. Below it the charcoal burns fiercely, turning almost white-hot. Above the grid is an iron hood which funnels off most of the smoke, allowing just a whiff to escape and reach the diners' nostrils. Larger fish such as bream and turbot are grilled using fish-shaped wire cages into which they are clamped, making it easy to turn them over without breaking. Anchovy, sardines and tunny fillets are barbecued on the grill itself. For more serious occasions, the Chuecas visit one of the three or four local restaurants. Certainly all their best business agreements are made at tables in such places. Here a dish called *Txangurro al horno* reigns supreme, having become another of the most representative dishes of this cuisine.

In the Basque Country, some people call spider crab, *txangurro*, others use the word to describe the common crab or buey, but in either case for this it is stuffed and baked.

 To make **Txangurro al horno**, baked spider crab, you need a very fresh spider crab weighing about 750 g (1 ½ lbs), ½ a medium-sized onion, finely chopped, 1 clove of garlic, 4 heaped tablespoons of tomato sauce, 1 carrot peeled and finely sliced, ½ a glass of Spanish brandy, ½ a glass of *txakolí* or fino sherry, ½ a glass of meat stock, 3 tablespoons of olive oil and a little chilli powder, breadcrumbs and a knob of butter. Bring to the boil a large pan of fresh water with a pinch of salt and a bay leaf. When the water comes to the boil put in the crab and boil for about fifteen minutes. Take out of the water, allow to cool a little and begin to remove the legs from the body and the latter from its shell. Use a kitchen hammer to open the legs, remove all the meat and then take out the meat from the main shell in the same way. Set aside the soft parts and contents of the shell. Shred the white meat and reserve it. Heat the oil in a frying-pan, add the onion

and carrot, cook until they are soft, then transfer to an earthenware dish and add the contents of the main shell; you can
also add some small pieces of shell from the legs which add
a good flavour, together with the tomato sauce, the wine,
the brandy and then flambé. Add the meat stock, chilli and
a little chopped parsley. Cook all of this together for about
fifteen minutes and then put through a sieve. Mix the resulting
sauce with the white meat which had been reserved previously
and return to the heat for a few minutes longer. Finally, use
this mixture to fill the shell, sprinkling a few breadcrumbs
on top and then put it in the oven at 220°C (425°F, gas mark
7) for seven minutes or until it is lightly browned.

Gone are the days when buying or selling the wine in Pedro's
old cellar was sealed on a firm handshake. Nevertheless, it is still
here that he spends his happiest moments, with his old seafaring
friends, discussing politics, money or perhaps his continual dis-
agreement with the incumbency of the church next door. Everything else he leaves in his sons' hands. They may be in Madrid
today, in Bilbao tomorrow. Pedro himself cares little about the
size of profit. He says that he will die happy simply in the knowledge that the word *txakolí* will not disappear from the dictionary
for a while.

THE CITY HOUSEWIFE

The life of Carmen Belandia, mother and housewife, seems to have little in common with those of her mother and grandmother. While their lives revolved around their families and homes, Carmen's is that of a modern, city woman; while they knew their place and rarely had a chance to express their views, she well knows her role in life and is determined to be heard and make a contribution to her country and its people. She has the strength and energy of Basque women in general. Sometimes rather brusque, at other times she is very tender. Above all, she is *koskera*. This is the name given to those born in the calle 31 de Agosto, the oldest street in San Sebastián, which runs between the churches of Santa María and San Vicente, *la parte vieja*, the old quarter. Carmen's family have lived in this street for more than a hundred years, and she, as well as most of her brothers and sisters, were born there. It was the only street which survived the great fire which broke out in 1813, when the French and English troops were fighting each other over the territory, and is too narrow to be used by cars or even bicycles. Houses and blocks of flats three or four stories high with balconies and shutters and steep staircases fashioned from well-polished wood, line both sides. Many date from the nineteenth century, with peeling ochre paint and stone facades. Practically all of them are occupied at ground level by bars, restaurants and gastronomic societies which keep it lively and noisy, especially at weekends, for twenty-four hours of the day.

But to be *koskera*, means much more than simply having been born in this street. It is a way of life, even a philosophy, shared not only by those who live there, but also by all who inhabit the tightly packed rectangle of streets looking on to the castle, the quay, and beyond it, the promenade with its bandstand made of wrought iron and multicoloured glass, where the town band plays on Saturdays. To be *koskera* means also to have grown up with the street's endless childrens' games – hopping, cops and robbers, and dreading the terrible moment when your mother shouted from the balcony for you to come up for supper. It also means loving the port, which in the olden days was a funfair of lovable characters, shopping in the La Brecha market, and knowing all the shopkeepers and regulars in the local cake shop and bar.

Carmen, known to her friends as Kika, her husband, José Ramon and their three sons, live on the sixth floor of an elegant block of flats dating from the thirties with impressive views of the sea and the city, which lies beyond the bridges separating the old town from the later suburbs. José Ramon who was born a doctor's son in the inland village of Legázpia, is a chemist who works in a paper factory on the outskirts of Pamplona. He is a calm, good natured man who loves music and the silence of the countryside. He is away during the week, leaving Kika with the children. Ivan the eldest, is studying chemistry at the Basque University, Igor is doing a technical engineering course at the College of Tolosa and little Aritz, who is seven, attends the local *Ikastola*, or Basque school.

Saturdays and Sundays are the only days when the family is complete and can meet around the kitchen table. Until six or seven years ago they had their meals in a little sitting-room which they had made in what was really the third bedroom, but the boys watched television all the time and things got out of hand so now they always eat in the kitchen, which is more homely and means less work for Kika. Breakfast is a leisurely affair, with large cups of milky hot chocolate, toast with butter and homemade jam from Kika's mother. Igor and Ivan often appear late in their pyjamas, sleepy-eyed after being out into the early hours with their friends. Afterwards, providing the weather is not too bad, José Ramon goes out for a long walk round the outskirts of San Sebastián. For him life would be unbearable without a few hours a week in contact with nature. It is the only way for him to relax after many long hard days, which, moreover, he spends away from his family. Often he takes Aritz with him and they catch up on the week that has gone by.

Kika goes out too, sometimes for a walk with friends, or perhaps to the opening of a new exhibition or a political demonstration. Usually she has lunch, the main meal of the day, well in hand before leaving, so that she will not have to worry about the time. Still wearing her dressing-gown, she quickly makes her preparations while breakfast is being cleared away. Although she prefers traditional Basque cooking, many of her dishes are influenced by her mother, a native of Castile, so she has always included in her menus some hybrid recipes which really cannot be considered typical of the region, but which she has modified in some way in order to find what pleases the rest of her family most and what also has a Cantabrian flavour. 'For example,' she explains, 'my rice dishes unlike those from other parts of the Peninsula, don't contain any sort of spices, not even saffron, which is becoming fashionable once again, and I wouldn't dream of using paprika or *pimentón*.'

 For **Arroz de pescado y marisco** for eight people she cleans ¼ kg (9 oz) of fresh squid carefully and cuts them into slices. Then she brings to the boil 200 g (7 oz) of good-sized fresh prawns, or Dublin Bay prawns if they are a reasonable price. She also puts ¼ kg (9 oz) of large clams, the sort that are used for clams in a green sauce, in salted water so that they will open and shed all the impurities they may contain. The other ingredients are ½ a chopped peeled onion, 6 cloves of garlic, peeled and chopped, 1 green pepper, 3 fresh tomatoes, peeled and chopped, 1 small tin of peas and 3 cups of rice. Later, when she has to add the liquid, she will use the same cups to measure out the reserved prawn stock to cook the rice. She pours a little virgin olive oil into a large earthenware *cazuela* and adds the onion, then the cloves of garlic and the green pepper, which she breaks in pieces with the hand. Next she puts in the squid and sautés everything together for three or four minutes. At this point she turns off the heat and covers the *cazuela* with a metal lid. For the final cooking, about twenty minutes before they are ready to eat, she will add the rice, sprinkling it in evenly with her hand. Using a wooden spoon she turns it in the oil to be sure that each grain has been coated, then stirs in the tomato and a pinch of salt, and pours in 2 cups of hot prawn stock for each cup of rice she has already added. After ten minutes gentle simmering she will add the clams and leave it to cook for another ten minutes, although rather more slowly. Just before serving she will arrange the prawns.

By half-past two they are all gathered around the table. The rice is cooked perfectly and Kika has put the *cazuela* in the middle of the table on a circular wooden mat, which protects the cloth. As always there is a bottle of wine, a jug of water and a basket of bread, which José Ramon has brought back from his walk, as well as several plates for them to put the shells on. Everyone is hungry and although they are talking as well, it is only a matter of minutes before they are ready for the next course. Kika loads the plates into the dish-washer at the same time as she brings steak and roasted peppers.

For Kika these family moments are all too short, the very essence of life. 'One of the most enjoyable things in my life were the family get-togethers at my mother's house after lunch and supper, when we would discuss our problems, share them, and try to solve them, or just talk about the day's happenings, or the lady who lived on the floor below. Unfortunately, this custom has now been lost in her house in Aldamar. Here I have tried putting course after course on the table to see if I could hold on to the boys longer to get into the habit of these conversations, but it never works. There are always other things – a football match, a friend to see, a meeting – pulling everyone off in other directions'.

All too soon, the weekend is over, having spent Sunday in the same relaxed and familiar mood as Saturday. During the weekend, if she has a little free time, Kika cooks a selection of small cakes from a recipe given to her by her friend Milagros from Tolosa, which is very popular with the boys. The cakes can be made with either flaky pastry, or else *pâte sucrée*, which, if this is possible, makes them even more delicious. Kika makes a sweet, enriched pastry which does not require the use of a rolling pin, though it must be rested in the refrigerator for twenty-four hours before use.

 To make **Pastelitos de fruta** you need for six to eight people 400 g (14 oz) of pastry, 1 kiwi fruit, 16 strawberries (small and whole if possible), 100 g (3½ oz) of raspberries, 1 banana, 3 apricots, a little fruit jam for the glaze and confectioner's custard. Make the pastry cases and cook them for about ten minutes in a relatively hot oven. Once they are cooked, fill them with a little confectioner's custard which has been flavoured with lemon and orange zest and a cinnamon stick. Peel the chosen fruit, cut it into small slices and brush them with a little jam which has been slightly heated.

On Monday, life returns to normal. José Ramon leaves home just before seven and, one by one, the boys set off to their schools. Until a few months ago Kika would take Aritz to catch the school bus.

It is nine o'clock and Kika has begun to clear the breakfast table. Half an hour later Mari, the daily help who comes every weekday, arrives and the work really begins. The two women take up carpets, make beds, air the rooms and change the bath-towels. For Kika, as for most Spanish women, the cleanliness of her home is very important, in spite of all the other important things in Kika's life which make it different from her mother's, loving and caring for her family is top of her list of priorities as a woman and mother.

Soon it is time to go to the market, La Brecha, only two streets away from the door. Without this daily visit to the market Kika could not conceive of cooking. No frozen food enters her house and it almost goes without saying that she has neither a freezer nor a microwave. She buys meat, chicken and fruit every two or three days, and gets anything else on a daily basis as she needs it from La Brecha. She has been shopping here since she was a child, as did her mother before her. Her father's mother, a sturdy woman with a large bun, used to have a fish stall here. She would leave home every day with two aprons and two sets of white cuffs so that she could change before returning home with an enormous basket, in which she would take back fish for the family. Every day, except Sunday, she would rise at five in the morning to go to the port of Pasajes, where the daily fish auction was held; and then be back in the city by seven o'clock to get her stall ready.

Two of Kika's sisters are still stallholders. They sell fresh and dried flowers from two adjacent stalls in the main market-hall. Flowers also constitute an important part of the day's shopping and not only are the stalls always decorated with them, but most women buy a small bunch or two, a couple of times a week. Kika always buys from the same stalls. She never asks the price since she is more concerned about the quality, and the person serving her knows this. All the customers and stallholders are on christian-name terms. She stops first at the stalls of the country people who have come down from the mountains or made their way in from the valley, with their great baskets of vegetables, fresh greens, flowers, cheeses, honey and beans. They occupy a special area built for them many years ago next to the market-hall proper. A pitched roof protects them from the rain, but not from the cold or the wind. From some counters, adorned with large checked cloths, home made produce are sold – rings of white bread, large chocolate or jam-filled buns, honey and cheese. Others simply sell greens and root vegetables. Some farmers' wives arrange their wares on a kind of long bench where, at the appropriate time, they can also sit down. Kika always buys from Ursula, whose chicory, silver beet, borage, artichokes and spinach – all grown in her own kitchen-garden – are the best to be found in the market. Each of them was still rooted in the ground only a few hours ago.

Then Kika makes her way towards one of the numbered stalls in the main building which specializes in golden maize-fed chickens but which also sells ham, smoked salmon fillets, quail's eggs and even daisies. Next, she stops at Carlo's butcher stall, which specializes in beef and veal and sells excellent calf's liver, the only kind that Ivan will eat. Here too, there are flowers, this time they are red roses but just for decoration. The cleanliness of the stalls throughout the market is impeccable.

Other stalls are relatively recent. There have always been herbalists, but wholefood stalls as we know them are still finding their feet. There has been one here for barely two months selling soya beans and wholemeal biscuits, but still relying on the old-fashioned goods, like manzanilla, camomile, mint tea, lime, flowers, oregano and thyme in glass jars, breads sold from round hemp baskets and molasses yeast for the bulk of its trade. Above, where the number of the stall is written, there is a large hand-written notice, 'Butter from El Roncal in Stock'.

In recent years the market, like many in Spain, has begun to feel the effects of the change of attitude and life-style of women. Kika says that only a few years ago she would never have believed that such problems could affect the markets of Euskadi. But increasingly as women go out to work it is becoming impossible for them to go to the market each day. Moreover, the prices in the supermarkets where they go once or twice a week for convenience, are competitive and even here, where people often ask for a certain quantity without having worked the price out in advance, this is beginning to be important. At the same time the council has raised the rents of the market stalls several times, leaving the stall-holders with ever narrowing profits.

Once Kika has finished her shopping, she goes to have coffee with her sisters at a little café opposite the market. They catch up on the news, talk about the children, and the *aitas*, parents. The five Belandia siblings, four sisters and one brother Patxi, are very close. All the sisters, except for one who married and now lives in Scandinavia, live in and around the old quarter and hardly a week goes by without them going out together, sometimes two of them, sometimes three. Although each has a life of her own they still need each other, just as years ago when they shared their lives and their room. All are active members of the same nationalist party and all are good cooks who think it essential to feed their families well. They claim though, that none of them has inherited the magic touch of their *amachu*, mother, who taught them to cook.

The highlights of Kika's culinary repertoire are dishes which belong to traditional cookery. These are the ones which José Ramon likes best. One is a *cocido*, a ubiquitous dish in which meat, sausages, vegetables and chickpeas simmer together to make a soup for a first course, followed by the chickpeas which are usually served with the other vegetables, and then meat and sausages, usually accompanied by a tomato, or tomato and pimiento sauce. In Kika's family they always called it the miracle of the loaves and fishes because, although there were so many of them, there was always enough and some left over. There was never much meat though, since times were hard.

In Kika's recipe, unlike those of many villages in Castile or Andalucía, the chickpeas do not play the main part. She only includes them because it is the done thing. Nor does she add fatty ingredients such as bacon, or even black pudding, or spicy *chorizo* sausage. The *cocido* can be made in a pressure-cooker to save time, but Kika does not like doing this since the flavour is not the same.

 To make **Cocido**, Kika takes a large stew-pot of water, to which she simply adds 2 or 3 cups of seasonal chickpeas, 2 sliced leeks, 1 onion, 2 carrots, 2 large bones and ½ kg (1 lb) of shin or stewing beef, and leaves it to cook for about two hours. Once it is cooked she strains it and puts back some of the carrot and leek with the soup. A few minutes before serving the broth she adds a few noodles which the boys particularly like.

 To make the **Tomato sauce** she puts into a frying-pan 2 table-spoons of olive oil and with the oil still cold, she adds ½ a chopped onion and 2 chopped cloves of garlic and when they begin to brown she adds 3 large peeled and chopped tomatoes; if she has no fresh tomatoes she uses a ½ kg (1 lb) tin. She leaves the sauce to cook slowly until the oil separates from the tomato and settles on the surface which normally takes about half an hour. At this point she transfers it to an earthenware dish with the meat, from which she has already removed any small pieces of fat and which she has cut up using an electric carving knife, to prevent it from breaking up. Sometimes, if she has had time to roast them, she adds some red peppers. She peels them and cuts them into strips. She sets aside the chickpeas, having dressed them with garlic and the oil in which it was fried.

Kika's favourite chickpea recipe is a rice one. I should point out that this is not really a typically Basque dish, but her father used to make it very well and she has inherited the recipe from him. She puts the chickpeas in quite a large cooking pot of boiling, salted water and adds a little garlic, leek and carrot. When the chickpeas are tender she adds the rice. Separately in a frying-pan, she makes a fried mixture of onion, tomato and garlic, which she then adds to the chickpeas and rice, which by then have absorbed any remaining water. Traditionally this should be eaten with a spoon in one's right hand and a piece of raw onion in the other.

  'My mother cooks meat dishes perfectly,' claims Kika, 'but when it comes to fish it is *el aita*, our father, who wins the prize. He inherited from his mother her love of sea food and when we were children he used to make us marvellous dishes, particularly from fish such as John Dory and monkfish, which in those days were looked down upon.'

For **Sopa de pescado** you need 1 French stick loaf, 1 monkfish weighing ½ kg (1 lb), 200 g (7 oz) of prawns, 200 g (7 oz) of clams, 3 medium sized onions, 2 cloves of garlic, ½ kg (1 lb) of tomatoes, 2 leeks, 1 glass of brandy and 2 litres (3½ pints) of water. In a stew-pot make a stock by simmering a leek and an onion, peeled and cut into chunks, with the well-cleaned fish. Strain the fish and vegetables and reserve the stock. Put a little olive oil in a casserole with a peeled and finely chopped onion, which should be fried until well browned, then add the glass of brandy. Next cut the bread into pieces and sauté this using a wooden spoon to turn it in the oil. Pour in the fish stock, making sure that the bread is covered, reduce to a low heat and leave to cook for an hour, adding more stock if the bread mixture looks too thick. Meanwhile, boil and peal the prawns and soak the clams in salted water to purge impurities. Put a little oil in a frying-pan with 2 cloves of garlic, 1 chopped leek and the vegetables from the stock. Sauté until lightly browned and then add the tomato, peeled and chopped, and cook until soft. Then purée and add gradually to the bread mixture, mixing well and simmering for five minutes. At this stage add the fish which has been cut into pieces and the bones and skin removed, the clams, already purged and the prawns. Leave it all to cook until the clams open, then remove from the heat. The dish is much better when made the day before it is needed.

While the men in Kika's family have always loved cooking and talking about food, it only has a relative importance for José Ramon, her husband, who is not in the habit of cooking. This is something rather unusual in the Basque Country and Kika often complains that while his parents took great care bringing up their children, they dedicated little time to eating well and to conversation around the table. The only thing that he excels in are the river crayfish that he often buys on a Friday in a little market on the outskirts of Pamplona. The whole family love this dish and, since there never seems to be enough for everybody, they all dip into the pot, trying to peel the crayfish as quickly as possible so that they will be in time for another one. 'Whenever José Ramon cooks this dish I have to change the tablecloth twice', remarks Kika.

To prepare **Cangrejos en salsa** you need for four people 1 kg (2 lbs) of crayfish, 1 large onion, about 6 ml (1 pint) of tomato sauce, a bay leaf, 1 glass of white wine, 1 glass of brandy, a little tabasco sauce, olive oil and salt. José Ramon prepares the crayfish in a large casserole, where he sautés the chopped onion until golden brown and then adds the crayfish; these are still alive and he washes them before adding to the dish. He sautés them with the onion and then adds the rest of the ingredients. He simply leaves the dish to cook for about fifteen minutes and then serves it accompanied by a hearty red Rioja wine.

In the fifties Kika caught tuberculosis and had to spend four months in bed and almost a year confined to the house. If there is anything that sticks in her mind about that year, it was that she really learned to like green vegetables, which were then practically never eaten in the Basque Country. In those days, the only vegetables people would eat were stewed butter beans, chickpeas and lentils. When the doctor prescribed greens for health reasons, patients would protest vociferously, saying that such things were only suited to animals. The pattern changed only fifteen years ago and Kika protests that today Basques still do not cook vegetables properly, boiling them far too long. She usually serves them al dente with one or two potatoes.

For **Espinacas con béchamel**, spinach in a béchamel sauce, she allows 1 kg (2 lbs) of spinach or silver beet. To make the béchamel which Kika prepares in the traditional Spanish way with olive oil rather than batter and flavoured onion, she heats 2 tablespoons of olive oil in a heavy based metal pan and adds 1 tablespoon of chopped onion. When the onion is golden-brown she adds 1 or 2 tablespoons of flour. Then she removes the pan from the heat and allows the flour to cool, before starting to add the milk, so that the flour will not form lumps and spoil the sauce. She adds the milk gradually, a little at a time, never measuring but judging by eye. Once it has been absorbed by the flour, she adds a little more and so on until the required thickness is achieved. At that stage, it is very important to allow the sauce to cook for about ten minutes, stirring all the time with a wooden spoon to prevent it from sticking, which it is prone to do. For croquettes of any sort, fish or meat, or for filling the *piquillo* peppers she prepares (and are delicious stuffed with prawns), she uses 2½ tablespoons of flour for 1 litre (1¾ pints) of milk.

Kika is also very concerned to hand down to her children her family's love of good food and cooking. Some nights, when she goes out, or if she is busy, the two eldest brothers take charge of getting the supper, which is usually something easy to prepare such as a soup to be warmed through, steak with fried potatoes and a little onion and tomato salad. Igor is not really interested in cooking, although he likes quantities of food, especially chips- but Ivor already knows how to make several good meals and often observes attentively while his *amachu* uses this or that ingredient to improve the flavour. He is fairly choosy about what he likes to eat and comes home for lunch because he claims that the meals at the university are a disaster. On the other hand he has no intention of becoming a member of a gastronomic society as his grandfather and uncle Patxi would wish. He likes to make dishes which are quick and require no fuss. One of his favourites is calf's liver with onion, a recipe that he learnt from Kika.

 To prepare **Higado de ternera encebollado** you need for four people ½ kg (1 lb) of calf's liver cut into tiny pieces, 2 large onions chopped very finely, olive oil and salt. Kika puts some olive oil into a large frying-pan and adds the onion, which she leaves to cook slowly for about thirty minutes until it is soft and almost caramelized. In a different pan she fries very lightly the liver and puts the pieces once ready into the pan with the onions, where they will cook together for a further two minutes. 'It would be a shame to overcook it', adds Kika. In my own recipe I add ½ a glass of *palo cortado* sherry to the onions before adding the liver.

Kika is also a member of one of the committees which deal with much of the day-to-day running of Aritz's school. Meals occupy an important place amongst the committee's concerns as it controls the contract for school lunches, which are made by an outside catering company and brought ready to serve in little trays. The menus offer a wide variety of recipes and ingredients in the traditional style, and at the same time are balanced from the nutritional point of view. One day they may have macaroni with meat sauce and chicken breast, followed by fruit; while on another it could be steak with chips and a chocolate dessert. Nonetheless, Kika and the other parents worry about the level of additives in ready-made products and would like to see more old-fashioned first courses of pulses, pasta and fresh vegetables, as well as more fruit to replace the packaged desserts.

Nevertheless, for all her emphasis on the importance of tradition, Kika is only too aware that her children are growing up in a very different world to that of their parents and must be left to find their own path. Likewise, the parallels between her life and that of the women of earlier generations are few and far between. Perhaps in some ways, her busy days are closer to those of her grandmother, who had the pride and independence of her fish stall in the market, than those of her *amachu* or mother. Kika says that her mother spent all her life at home, and in a way has become rather sad and quiet. The Civil War with its tragic consequences, had left her deeply scarred, as though numbed, and she took care of her home and children silently. Kika remembers the household suffering all kinds of privations, including hunger. She can still recall the colour of the ration-cards and the hours spent queuing interminably for practically nothing, or just a few pieces of dark bread.

In her own life, Kika attempts to find a compromise between tradition, which she will struggle with all her might to defend,

and the personal fulfilment that she needs to go on living from
day-to-day. She enjoys looking after her home and family, just
as her mother and her grandmother did, and would never abandon
it, but she always feels the need to do more. At present Kika does
not go out to work. Until a few months ago she used to work
in a friend's clothes shop, but this meant that she lost her freedom
and so she decided to give it up. 'I am already over forty and
I don't want my life to fly past without spending some of my
time doing the things which really matter,' she says passionately,
'such as fighting against the construction of a tower block which
would shut off our view to the sea, or attending political meetings
and discussions.'

Like her grandmother, she lives a city life and goes out every
day to meet family and friends. On Friday evenings she and José
Ramon always go out together with friends. In winter they usually
go to a cider house in Astigarraga and Kika is responsible for taking
some meat which she buys in the market in the morning. They
sort out their expenses afterwards, at the end of the evening in
a little bar where they have coffee and a brandy. In summer they
usually go to one of the little villages along the coast to eat fish
grilled in the open air. She adores to share such moments with
José Ramon and their friends, to chat with them all, to enjoy the
cider or *txakolí*.

Like many of her generation, Kika also revels in the traditional
fiestas which have not yet disappeared. Every year she and José
Ramon go to Tolosa for the Carnival celebrations, which here
become bigger every year while in most Basque towns they have
almost gone forever. The celebrations run over a whole week and
involve a great deal of eating and drinking, especially on *Jueves
Gordo*, Fat Thursday. *Chorizo* is offered free of charge in all the
bars as an appetizer, and in the restaurants, gastronomic societies
and private homes they make a dish called *picacha*, using onion,
lamb's blood and intestine. After Fat Thursday, comes *Viernes Flaco*,
Thin Friday, so called because after the previous day's excesses
most people feel somewhat under the weather and rest their stomach for a day which is followed by a normal Saturday. Then

at last it is Carnival Sunday, announced by the *alborada, audade* or dawn music at six o'clock in the morning, when the *txistularis* play in every square. 'Get up early, today is fiesta', they sing all round the town. As well as the official ceremonies, there are others – sometimes a play or a float that travels around the streets – devised by different groups of friends who have been rehearsing for months in great secrecy.

A few months later, at the end of June, Kika, José Ramon and the children go back to Tolosa to celebrate St John's Eve at the small *caserío* of their old friends Asensio and Milagros. Until a few years ago, Asensio was the proprietor of the paper-works, a traditional industry in the area which declined in recent times, but now he publishes Basque language books on culture. He is especially interested in the ancient pagan rites in honour of water and fire and every year invites friends to celebrate St John's Eve just as their primitive forbears would have done with a feast and bonfire. Although the Roman Catholic Church appropriated these ceremonies, they were originally pagan and date from long before Christian times. In days gone by weeks were spent building bon-fires using timber, shrubwood and a great trunk of bay representing the branches which were blessed on Easter Sunday. The fires could be seen burning from a distance, twenty or even thirty of them in front of the doorways of the *caseríos* and even in the town streets, their flames consuming a rag guy, which had been made from old clothes, and who represented any evil spirit which had lodged there during the past year or might do so in the future.

Asensio engages a neighbour to organize everything for the occasion, from the huge bonfire to a system of poles and ropes which will be used to roast the kid, in a similar way to that used in the caves of Zagarramurdi (described in my chapter on *The Tradition of the Kaiku-Maker*). Afterwards they usually have a good cheese which Asensio buys from a shepherd in the Aralar moun-tains.

Kika is a modern woman who has kept inside the love for her family, for Euskadi, for friendship and for her town. The way of life she grew up with, including her family's political beliefs, has remained with her as it was with her ancestors. You can see her as a woman of today who often goes to demonstrations which manifest themselves in several different ways: processions with giant carnival figures and representations of Basque folklore; impassioned speeches in the Plaza de la Constitución sometimes in Basque, sometimes Castilian, with excited speakers trying to make a point; or dancing crowds with traditional music. She is caught in a cross-flow of tradition and modern beliefs in which, until now, the traditional values have had the upper hand.

THE GASTRONOMIC
SOCIETIES

Luciano Belandia, Kika's father, has been a member of a gastronomic society all his life. A proud cook admired by men and women
alike, his expertize has been honed over many years cooking two
or three nights a week at the society for male friends. When he
was younger and his work as a taxi driver gave him the odd free
hour, he would drop by at other times too, to play a round of
mus, a card game rather like whist. Now that he is retired he spends
two or three hours a day there.

Luciano is not unusual. The societies, where men gather to eat,
cook, play cards or organize various cultural and sporting activities,
are to be found all over the Basque Country. Some clubs have
only a few dozen members, others a couple of hundred. There
are clear cut differences too between those of the various Basque
provinces – Guipúzcoa, Alava and Vizcaya – both in the cooking
and in the different types of activities to which the societies are
commited. Those of Vizcaya, for example, are said to be more
class-orientated. But broadly speaking all the societies run along
the same lines. Each society has a headquarters where small groups
of members or *cuadrillas*, each with their own cook or cooks, get
together frequently for a drink or an evening meal. Bricklayer and

government minister sit down together at the same table, to eat from the same dish and to share the same loaf of bread. Everybody is addressed in the familiar *tu*, rather than the formal *usted* form. As they would put it, every man is a nobleman. Each society has a number of by-laws governing many of their activities. New members have to be proposed by one of the existing members. A secret ballot is held by placing marbles in a little box; white for yes and black for no. If, when the count is made, not all the marbles are white, there is no hope for the prospective candidate, whoever may have proposed him.

Women have always been barred from becoming members, although now they may sometimes be invited to lunch on a week-day. Recently, for example, there was a major controversy even in the national press, after a well-known society refused to admit a female politician to a business dinner being held there. At Amaika-bat, Luciano's society, women are admitted to the dining-room in the afternoon, but only with prior permission. What they may never do is set foot inside the kitchen. The only women allowed there are employed staff like a female cook who assists the members of larger societies on a regular basis and looks after the kitchen. With Basque men learning to share some of their leisure time with their wives, something to which they would never have confessed previously because it would have been seen as a sign of weakness, there is talk of change, and a small number of mixed societies have been formed. But the change is likely to be slow, for all the members of a society have to be in agreement for the rules to alter.

The societies and their laws date back to the nineteenth century although there is much debate over their precise origins. The first one started when a group of friends in liberal, mercantile nine-teenth-century San Sebastián leased some premises in the old part of the city to cook and drink unaffected by the opening and closing hours of the cider houses. Each member had a key to the building and the larder, and everyone was considered trustworthy. But the societies' roots lie deeper than that. Many people maintain that they grew up, in spirit at least, after the destruction of San Sebastián by the English in 1813, during the Peninsular War. Wellington had ordered Graham to lay siege to the city, which was occupied by the French, and after several days of fighting, the Anglo-Portuguese Army succeeded in breaching the walls. Then, in the hour of glory, came the senseless destruction which seems inherent in the nature of war. A tired and confused army vented its rage on the very inhabitants of the fortress it had come to rescue: they murdered, pillaged and burned, remorselessly razing the city to the ground in only a few hours. With indomitable Basque spirit, groups formed to organize the rebuilding of the town. Their members came from very different strata of society; there were priests and fishermen, bakers and magistrates. United by circumstances, they treated each other as equals. Eventually, they met together to have a meal, to talk and to agree as to what should be done. Out of these meals, it is said, grew the spirit of the societies.

Others say that their appearance can only be explained by the particular political mood of the time. By mid-century the Basque Country, like the rest of Spain, was divided between, on the one hand, traditionalist Carlist thought, which supported an absolute monarchy and the old regional laws or *fueros*, and on the other, progressive liberalist thought, which backed a republic or monarchy with power enshrined in the Spanish constitution and a uniform legal code free from class and regional privileges. The rural Basques were unquestioning defenders of Carlism, but San Sebastián, a city of wealthy and important traders, devoted to amusement and friendship, certainly tolerant and perhaps even selfish, wanted to do away with the old problems of customs duties between regions and was strongly liberal. It was in this climate that the societies first made their appearance, offering a suitable open, egalitarian atmosphere for entertainment and conversation. Today, the majority and the best known of the societies are still those of San Sebastián.

There is another theory too. Julio Caro Baroja, a noted Basque ethnologist, has argued that the birth of the societies must be allied to the traditions of sailors, who, he believes, spent such long periods away from their families, that there was a natural dichotomy between the lives of women – wife, children, mother, mother-in-law – and those of men. Each sex has his or her place, the women in the home and the man elsewhere. According to his view, the societies would have emerged against the background of the port with its bars and cider houses and on this was founded the concept of the importance of cooking and sharing meals. There is certainly some truth behind the idea of a dichotomy. Even today, it is not thought unusual that men should prefer the company of male friends to that of their nearest and dearest, and they themselves say that they do not only congregate to eat and cook but also to go in search of peace and quiet, the lack of the need to give explanations, or to make any sort of an effort. Nevertheless, the kitchen is the main pivot around which the societies revolve. At Amaika-bat, Luciano's society in the old town of San Sebastián, the kitchen dates back to the early thirties when the club moved to the premises. Here, eight enormous gas stoves and two hot-plates meet the needs of the current membership of 140. Beyond the cooking area are endless formica storage cupboards. The part of the kitchen which adjoins the dining-room proper is open-plan so that everybody can see what is going on in the holy of holies all the time. Above the stoves is an enormous black iron hood which extracts the smoke and smells.

Most of the ingredients in the kitchen larder are packed in small quantities, just the right amount for one session. For example, the oil is packed in quarter-litre bottles, and similarly the flour, sugar and the rest of the basic ingredients are measured out. When one of the members has finished cooking he clears up and jots down in the notebook what he has used that day and then pays. Nobody keeps account and there is never any money missing when the member in charge of the shopping collects the money needed for more ingredients.

Normally, society cooks prepare recipes that have been passed down orally from the farmhouse kitchen, the *caserío*, and the food of the fisherman. They understand the basics of traditional Basque cookery, learned instinctively, which they have added to with the passing of the years. What they attempt to do, perhaps the most difficult thing of all, is to make a personal contribution, but to remain true to the spirit of the original recipe. Each cook's repertoire may only consist of three of four recipes, but he embroiders on them to make the most of what is in season, selecting the best quality produce for the dish, he often succeeds in creating the most elusive flavours that only patience and dedication, together with a real love of cooking and sharing, are capable of achieving. Here there is never any of the hurry you find in the professional kitchen. Dishes are talked of with affection. The cook takes his time and enjoys cooking for himself and even more for others.

Luciano's specialities are all based on fish. Two dishes which are particular favourites with his group of fellow members are scrambled eggs with anchovies and gilthead in fisherman's style. Luciano finds cleaning the anchovies so tiresome, that he buys them from one of the little stalls outside the doors of the Brecha market where the fishermen's wives sell them ready to cook. Best of all are the tiny ones, to be found on sale once or twice a year, which are prepared in the following way.

 For a **Revuelto de anchoas** take a clove of garlic, leave it unpeeled, but cut a slit around the middle so that the flavour is extracted. Put a little olive oil in a frying-pan and in it fry the garlic clove until golden. Remove it and then put in the anchovies and cook on a low heat; a little chilli can be added to give them a special appeal. When they are cooked pour in the number of beaten eggs required, one or two for each person. Do not allow them to set too much. One of the secrets of this is to eat it immediately it is cooked.

Luciano thinks that gilthead bream is very reasonable in price compared with other fish, and cooks it often at the society following a recipe passed on to him by a sailor friend of his fathers.'

 To prepare **Gilthead bream** he firstly cleans the fish carefully, then poaches it in a little salted water. Meanwhile, in a casserole, he fries a small finely chopped onion, a chopped clove of garlic, 4 peeled and de-seeded tomatoes and a few sprigs of chopped parsley. When the onion is golden-brown, after about seven minutes, he seasons the mixture with salt and pepper, pours in a glass of white wine, preferably *txakolí*, which he allows to reduce to about half. He adds a little of the stock from poaching the gilthead and if available, 3 or 4 anchovies, which will contribute to the flavour. After cooking for about thirty-five minutes he strains the sauce, arranges the fish, which he has kept hot, on a serving dish and pours over the sauce.

Not all the dishes made by the society cooks are quite so traditional or straight forward. As a friend of mine from Zarauz explained, the society cook prepares the food with such tenderness that the professional chef may well find himself threatened more than once with competition. One of Amaika-bat's most renowned cook's recipes, for example, is red peppers stuffed with crab and prawns. This is an adaptation of a dish which with slight differences has leapt to fame in the hands of the region's *nueva cocina* chefs. While the societies adopt little from *nueva cocina*, if the truth be told, they eye it surreptitiously from time to time. In the following recipe the cook has substituted cream for milk, and used béchamel instead of flour to thicken the sauce, in accordance with the good practice of the society cook, who only used the bare minimum of flour to thicken his sauces, and where possible, none at all. The peppers in question, *pimientos del pico* or pointed peppers, named because of their shape, are small in size and slightly spicy. The best are the *piquillo* ones from the Llodosa area in Navarre. Although they are delicious fresh, they are more often found canned.

 To prepare **Pimientos rellenos** for six people the cook buys 18 *pimientos del pico*, 300 g (11 oz) of good-sized fresh prawns, 3 tablespoons of flour, 3 tablespoons of olive oil, 1 shallot, ½ litre (15 fl oz) of milk and a little salt. First he sets the oven at 180°C (350°F, Gas mark 4). He puts the unpeeled prawns to boil in a saucepan with plenty of water, simply bringing them to the boil, and then removes them. Any more cooking, he says, would dry them up too much. Meanwhile he begins to make a béchamel sauce using a frying-pan. First he uses the oil to sauté the shallot which he has chopped very finely. After a few seconds, when this is tender, he adds the flour and cooks until golden brown; then he removes the pan from the heat, so that once the flour mixture cools it will not go lumpy when the milk is added. Once the mixture is warm he adds the milk a little at a time and then returns the pan to the heat, allowing the liquid to be absorbed into the flour before the next addition. Next the mixture begins to thicken and he cooks it for about twenty minutes to ensure that the flour loses its flavour before removing from the heat. He peels the prawns, and since they are large, cuts them in half, and then adds them to the béchamel. Then he stirs in the white crab meat. When the mixture has cooled somewhat, he uses it to fill the peppers, which he arranges in an oven dish. Next he makes the sauce by mixing in a bowl a little milk, 2 table-spoons of the béchamel which were left over, 2 *piquillo* peppers, cut up finely, and a pinch of salt. He puts this through a sieve to form a very light sauce which he pours carefully over the peppers. The dish is then heated through in the oven for only about fifteen minutes, otherwise the peppers would dry up.

Luciano is particularly proud of Amaika-bat's renown for sporting activities. It is known for introducing hand-ball to the Basque Country, for its string hockey team and for its *traineras*, or small fishing boats propelled by oars, which have had innumerable successes in the races held in La Concha Bay. Sports and gastronomy may initially seem a strange mixture. In his book *Comer en Euskalherria*, Juan José Lapitz suggests it came about because in the forties, under the restrictive laws of Franco, the societies had to pretend that their main interest was something safer than political talk on a full stomach. A sport like *pelota* or rowing was the obvious choice.

Of course, since those days, the societies have changed a great deal. Until recently, many men went to them daily. Eating well and doing as one pleased went hand in hand and the societies constituted a working man's answer to the restaurant. But now costs have escalated and become so expensive that having a meal at the society every day is becoming too dear for the traditional member. Moreover, the membership fees of many societies are very high. Patxi Belandia, Luciano's son and Kika's brother, paid seven thousand pesetas to join his society, Gaztalupe, fourteen years ago, but now it costs forty thousand, and its annual subscription is seven thousand pesetas As a result of the prices and more general social changes, it is becoming increasingly difficult to attract young members, and the *cuadrillas* are begining to lose the mix of ages that they used to enjoy.

Nonetheless the societies are still greatly cherished. Patxi, for example, goes to Gaztalupe every day and cooks for his *cuadrilla* every Friday. It is a prestigious society and one of the largest. Usually on weekdays three or four members share the gas range, but on a Friday there may be as many as seven of them. Sometimes they cook in silence, and always without interfering in their companion's work. While Patxi is immersed in his task the rest of his *cuadrilla* go off to the bar opposite to have a drink. They are a group of twelve, the eldest of whom is in his seventies. Patxi in his early forties, is the youngest. When it is time to clear the tables they will help, but not to do the washing-up. They pay a woman who has been employed by the society to do that.

Patxi speaks of his cooking with the same precision that he manifests when he is actually doing it; he knows quantities, cooking times and oven temperatures by heart. He learned to cook by watching his *amachu* or mother, in the same way that most Basque men learn, whether they will admit it or not. He says that when he was young he would observe patiently how she made this or that dish and then he would reproduce it at the club, though adding his own ideas and style of doing things: this or that ingredient, a few minutes more or less, a bit of parsley. Normally, he works with a fixed price budget of about one thousand pesetas – or five pounds – per head, buying everything he needs at La Brecha market.

On special occasions, for example, when it is the birthday of one of the *cuadrilla*, or he is cooking for the *Gobierno Vasco*, the Basque Government, he gets the chance to spend a bit more and go to town. For these dinners he offers a number of *tapas* as an apéritif: ham, oysters, prawns, asparagus and mayonnaise. Carefully, he slices the cured ham, which is a slightly sweeter version than those ones from further south, and arranges this on a plate in the shape of a flower. He keeps the oysters bought that morning on ice and needs only to cut some lemon quarters when he is ready to serve them. He will cook the prawns on a hot-plate, only on one side, for a couple of minutes, and no more. The special fat, white asparagus spears, the sort that come only seven or nine to the tin, must be the Horlando brand, his favourite. To make his mayonnaise, he puts two egg yolks in a bowl and begins to add a thin stream of olive oil. The wooden spoon turns tirelessly, the cook stirs on without changing his rhythm or stopping, or the mayonnaise might separate. It thickens and grows into a shiny mass in silence. Nothing must interrupt the cook's concentration. Once he has obtained the required quantity he will whisk the egg whites until stiff and fold them into the sauce to lighten it, together with a few drops of lemon juice and a pinch of salt.

 For the last dinner he cooked, the first course was a **Sopa de fideos y carne**. The main ingredients for this are a piece of shin beef weighing ¼ kg (9 oz), 2 thin leeks, 1 carrot and 1 onion. He fills a cooking-pot with 2 litres (3½ pints) of water and adds all the ingredients, then puts it on the heat for about an hour. At this stage he will remove the meat, clean it up and sieve the other ingredients, before adding them back into the stock, together with 150 g (5 oz) of *fideos*, fine noodle-like pasta. To finish off the soup he will hard-boil 2 eggs in another saucepan and chop them and the meat very finely. This garnish is added to the soup just before serving and gives it an excellent texture.

Patxi, like his father, prefers cooking fish to meat dishes, particularly hake and fresh cod in casseroles and sauces. He also likes to fry hake. 'It may appear very simple', he says with a smile, 'but I think that frying fish correctly, particularly such a delicate fish as hake, requires a great deal of care and expertize.'

On the stove he heats a heavy, iron frying-pan containing quite a lot of olive oil. 'The right temperature is essential', he maintains. Egg-coated hake fillets cut into relatively small pieces of about 50 g each (2 oz) lie on a wooden board. Unlike some cooks Patxi uses only beaten egg to coat them, insisting that flour spoils the fine texture of hake. He adds two unpeeled cloves of garlic, and fries them quickly until golden, removes them and takes the frying-pan off the stove for a few seconds as the oil has heated up rather more than he wishes. Then he begins to fry the fish. He cooks only five of the hake pieces at a time, because he does not want them to stick together. After two minutes on either side, he lifts them out with the fish slice and transfers them to a plate covered with a white linen cloth which will absorb any excess oil. It is very important that they should be cooked just enough, that is, moist in the middle, but certainly not oily. He will serve the fish with a lettuce, tomato and spring onion salad.

Another of his favourite dishes is monkfish in its cooking juices. This he varies according to the occasion and season. Here is a springtime version with fresh peas. Sometimes he follows the recipe but adds ten large prawns as a finishing touch. Of course, they make it a more expensive dish. Sometimes he uses hake instead of monkfish, and perhaps some *kokotxas* instead of the clams.

 The ingredients for **Rape en salsa** are 3 finely chopped cloves of garlic, 1 leek, 6 large clams and 6 pieces of monkfish, each weighing about 200 g (7 oz) each, fillets from the upper side of the fish, from which Patxi carefully removed the backbone. Half an hour before beginning to cook it he sprinkles salt over the fish and covers it with a cloth. This gives the fish a certain firmness which improves it by causing it to lose some of the water which it contains, explains the cook. He puts an aluminium casserole on the hotplate and pours a little oil into it; of course the oil must have an acidity level of 0.4 on the label! Then he adds the garlic and the leek, peeled and chopped and allows them to cook for about ten minutes, after which he adds the clams (they have previously been soaked in salted water to purge them), and once they have opened, he adds the pieces of fish. He rocks the dish gently from side to side, it would be a pity to add flour to thicken the sauce and so he goes on doing this for about ten minutes, sometimes putting the casserole on the heat, at others removing it for a few seconds. He turns each of the fish fillets over and continues the same process for about five minutes. Then he adds ¼ kg (9 oz) of tiny peas which he bought already out of the pods, cooks them for another five minutes and adds the chopped parsley, then he covers the casserole and takes it out to the table.

 The sweet dishes that Patxi prefers to make are simple fruit preparations which are very traditional in Euskadi. To prepare **Peras con vino**, fresh pears in red wine, you need 1 pear, not too soft nor juicy, weighing about 150 g (5 oz) each. The other ingredients are 2 bottles of fruity red wine, a cinnamon stick, a little cointreau, the juice of 2 oranges and ¼ kg (9 oz) of sugar. He peels the pears carefully and pours the wine into an oven dish to which he adds the cinnamon, the sugar and the mixture of liqueur and orange juice. Then he places the pears in the wine and puts them into the oven to cook for three-quarters of an hour at 180°C (350°F, Gas mark 4).

 Another of his favourite puddings is **Baked apples**. He chooses a good-sized apple for each person, washes and cores it, puts a little butter in the cavity, together with a small handful of currants and a tablespoon of sugar. He places the apples on an oven dish, adds a glass each of brandy and Marie Brizard liqueur and puts them into an oven pre-heated to 200°C (400°F, Gas mark 6). He cooks them until they puff up and are slightly browned, after which he puts them under the grill for a couple of minutes. The brandy gives them a very special colour and flavour.

Although Patxi learnt to cook from his mother, is happily married and fond of his sisters, he is adamant that the societies are right in barring women. 'It is quite enough that we already let them in at lunchtime. Dinner is quite another thing. Women always want to go where they are prohibited and the fact of the matter is that where societies have allowed them in, it doesn't work. Ten years ago we all decided to have mixed lunches every day, but the truth is that the women interfere absolutely everywhere, where they had no call to do so. It was questions all the time. "What does your husband do?", "You've bought a new car?" Worse still, they would come into the kitchen and talk nineteen to the dozen so that you couldn't concentrate so we stopped it in 1980. Now, once again, they are allowed in at lunchtime, but they rarely come, I don't know why.'

At three o'clock in the afternoon a member is sitting by himself playing Patience, another is rebottling the liqueur miniatures which were consumed during the week; only ten years ago he had to do this operation once a day. Without young people the future of the societies looks bleak but today they are still a stronghold of Basque character and for that there is hope. Not all Basque men belong to gastronomic societies, some of them have not the time or the inclination, nevertheless nearly all know how to cook. Patxi and Kika agree that one of the best cooks they know is Juan Cruz, who has never belonged to a gastronomic society. A dreamer and an adventurer whose favourite pastime is travelling, he says that he could never spend every evening in the same place, just as he could never settle into the routine of professional life as a lawyer. He prefers to share a good meal with his friends and frequently arranges spontaneous dinner or lunch parties on the spur of the moment. Juan lives surrounded by pictures and souvenirs, on the top floor of a beautiful old house in Calle 31 de Agosto, just a stone's throw from Kika's home. Although he has a small kitchen every detail in it is perfect. Nothing is missing: sharpened knives, all sorts of spices, a shelf full of vegetable preserves and fruit in different liqueurs that he prepares in the summer, oils flavoured with rosemary and thyme. On the terrace with its view of rooftops and church bell-tops pointing heavenwards, is a long marble trestle-table for summer parties and an *asador* or barbecue, where he can grill a nice bream or a dozen sardines fresh from the port. Inside are a solid-fuel stove which provides warmth on wintery days and pictures and souvenirs, plants and books.

Although Juan enjoys cooking traditional Basque food, his dishes are more open to outside influences than those of many other cooks. Curiously, he first learnt to cook in America, when a Basque friend found him a job as an assistant in the kitchen of a French restaurant close to New York. Later, he travelled down to South America and into the Amazon. 'The American experience is compulsive', he comments, 'And it calls us back over and over again through the centuries, to discover virgin territory. People are so much more sensitive in Latin America, more generous and intuitive. For example, in Chile people say when they are awaiting the arrival of the first strawberries, "Wait until it is time for the *durangos*. You will see; the little fruits will be ready in a fortnight's time." '

Cookery books are the source of some of his favourite recipes. From a recent acquisition he took this *millefeuille* of leeks, which in the photograph, at least, looked most impressive. He has added a few touches of his own to translate the written word into something truly delicious.

 For the filling of this **Hojaldre de puerros** Juan Cruz uses 5 large leeks, 2 peeled and chopped onions, 4 eggs, 1 soupspoon of flour, a pinch each of salt and pepper and a little leek stock. One can add a little single cream also. Once the leeks are clean and cut into thin rings, he puts them into cold water to cook until tender, but still holding their shape. He strains them and reserves the cooking water for later. In a frying-pan he sautés the onion in a little olive oil and when it begins to turn golden, he adds the cooked leeks. Then he mixes the flour into the cold leek stock and adds it to the onion and leek to form a béchamel mixture, which he cooks. If cream is to be used, this should be added before the sauce finishes cooking. Next the salt and pepper are added and the béchamel mixed with the lightly beaten eggs. He prepares a round, loose bottomed tin by covering the base with half the pastry, then pours the béchamel mixture carefully into the tin. When it is almost full, he covers the sauce with the remaining pastry, pinches together the edges and brushes the top with beaten egg so that it will brown. He puts the tin into the oven for half an hour at 180°C (350°F, Gas mark 4). After this he will turn the temperature up for another fifteen minutes, or until the dish proves to be juicy, but set, if pierced with a knife. With this he recommends a good *txakolí* wine from Guetaria.

Kika particularly likes Juan's recipe for a leg of lamb with a forcemeat of pork, pinekernels, chopped apple, egg, bread-crumbs and a drop of *txakolí*, which he once cooked for her and José Ramon.

 To prepare **Leg of lamb** Juan buys the leg already deboned and then the only thing he has to do is to prepare the forcemeat himself and stuff and tie-up the leg with string. It then goes into a moderate oven 170-190°C (400°F, Gas mark 6) with a little olive oil, just to help it brown for about three-quarters of an hour. He cuts up a couple of carrots, 2 cloves of garlic and a medium-sized onion, removes the joint from the oven and arranges them around it. He will leave it in a moderate oven for another 20 minutes. After this he will go back into the kitchen, remove the roasting dish from the oven, transfer the joint to a serving dish and put it in the second oven to keep warm. He will stir a little flour into the juice of the meat, add 2 cupfuls of meat stock and cook this for a few minutes more until it thickens. He will strain the sauce to remove the carrot and onion and then pour a little over the slices of meat on the individual plates, carefully carved by Kika.

When Juan makes traditional or classic dishes, he usually alters or adds to the recipe to suit his taste. Take as an example his version of *tocinos de cielo*, literally heavenly piglets, a kind of rich caramel custard, one of the most traditional of Basque sweets, also very popular in the rest of Spain and particularly in Andalucía. In order to counterbalance their extreme sweetness, he has made a light raspberry sauce, on which the *tocinos* sit.

To prepare the **Tocinos de cielo** you need 12 egg yolks, 350 g (12 oz) of sugar, ¼ litre (½ pint) of water, grated rind of ½ a lemon and for the sauce 250 g (8 oz) of fresh raspberries, 2 tablespoons of clear honey. Prepare a syrup by dissolving the sugar in the water. Place the mixture over the heat in a heavy-based saucepan and bring to the boil. Do not stir the syrup while it is boiling, otherwise crystals will form. Boil the sugar until it forms a small thread (103°C/218°F). Set aside using a little to line the moulds. Leave to cool slightly. Beat the egg yolks to a smooth consistency in a mixing bowl. Gradually add the sugar syrup, stirring continuously. Strain the mixture into the prepared mould or moulds. Cooking the *tocinos* is a tricky operation and should not be done in a *bain marie*. It can only be done by steaming. Bring the water to the boil and steam for about ten to fifteen minutes. Cooking time depends on the size of the mould used, but do not over-cook the *tocinos*. Make sure the moulds are quite cold before turning out.

Friendship and food, Kika believes, go together hand in hand. As far as she is concerned the greatest moments in life always take place around a table, without being in a hurry. It may be at home with your family, in the local restaurant, the gastronomic society or cider house, or in a bar sampling *pinchos*, or tapas while talking about the events of the day with a loved-one or friend.

Once a year in the middle of January, the gastronomic societies of San Sebastián open their doors to all visitors and women for the *Tamborrada*, probably the most important festival of the year, when small processions of drummers in military costumes and chef's whites parade during the entire night through the old part of the town. Each procession of soldiers and chefs, or *Tamborrada*, belongs to a gastronomic society. Often two of the groups will meet on a corner or crossroads and the already deafening sound will double, forcing the followers of each band to retreat into nearby bars for a drink.

The practice of holding marathon drumming sessions is quite common in Spain. Luis Buñuel, the Aragonese film-maker, gave a wonderful description of the drummers of the little town of

Calanda in his book *My Last Breath*: 'When the first bell in the church tower begins to toll, a burst of sound, like a terrific thunder-clap, electrifies the entire village, for all the drums explode at the same instant.' Contrary to that almost sad ritual, the drumming in San Sebastián is joyful and exuberant, but the rolling sound of the drums has the same explosive power.

The excitement and tension of the festival builds up during the course of the evening. Before the official opening of the fiesta in the Plaza de la Constitución at midnight, families and friends feast together, either at home, dining on traditional fried elvers and bar-bequed bream, in restaurants or in the gastronomic societies on a menu enthusiastically prepared by the team of cooks given the honour of cooking for this grand occasion. Patxi Belandia invariably spends all day at Gaztalupe cooking, Kika and José Ramon go to a restaurant for dinner while Igor and Ivor are out on the streets of the old town, seizing here a piece of potato ome-lette, there a pinch of cod or a portion of Russian salad. Many of the bars have restaurants attached to the main building, or at least places to sit and order several of the specialities normally listed on a black-board placed where all the eyes can see it. Prawns, salmon, tunny cooked with peppers, fried anchovies, Russian salad, cured ham, anchovy omelettes, meat balls, snails, tripe, calves' cheeks, small squid, scrambled eggs with wild mushrooms, scram-bled eggs with fresh garlic and spinach and quail in sauce figure among many others. A long night lies ahead and everyone eats plenty so that they will not be hungry later.

As midnight approaches, the crowds pack into the old Plaza de la Constitución. On a large platform in the centre stand the drummers, half of them soldiers and half cooks, facing outwards in single file around the edge. The clock strikes, and the soldiers, clad in nineteenth-century French army uniform, begin to play real drums while the cooks, dressed in white with aprons, a red handkerchief round their necks and a tall chef's hat, drum on small wooden barrels. Two conductors, one a soldier and one a chef, guide their respective bands. There are also seven cooks armed with an enormous wooden fork and seven soldiers with large pickaxes; they are led by a chef with the blue and white satin flag of the town and are drawn up opposite the civic dignitaries. The crowd's high spirits are infectious and every distracting sound is drowned out by the deafening, but compulsive sound of the drums. Even the Lord Mayor keeps time with the beat. The atmosphere is electric, the pride of the Basque people in its land and customs almost tangible. The drumming suddenly seems to pound on and on, followed by one of six rolls. The crowd starts launching a barrage of missiles such as potatoes, tomatoes and hard-boiled eggs at the Mayor. 'Well, it is our way of showing what we think of his performance as leader of the Town Council', explained one man. Traditions are always important.

There are many different stories about the history of the *Tamborrada*, but on one point everyone is agreed. Until about a hundred years ago, there were more soldiers than civilians occupying the walled city of San Sebastián. At five o'clock each morning, the city's bakers would fetch water from one of the town's public drinking fountains, while the changing of the guard took place. From time to time, half teasingly, they would beat out a rhythm on their pitchers and barrels to echo mockingly the guard's drums. There is little doubt that the cooks of the present-day parade represent those bakers.

Apparently, during the first fifty years in the history of the procession, the participants wore whatever came to hand. Then, one day a collection of old, early nineteenth-century French army uniforms fell into the hands of one of the gastronomic societies and they decided to wear these for the masquerade. By such degrees the present-day ritual evolved. However, the uniforms worn by the children for their drum parade, which takes place the following morning in the Plaza del Ayuntamiento overlooking La Concha, the shell-shaped bay, are a collection of more than forty different designs, including not only those of the French Army, but also ancient uniforms from many other countries.

Once the ceremony in the Plaza de la Constitución is over, the society's *tamborradas* leave the premises in an established order and the crowd follows the parade as they process through the streets.

From time to time a great crowd builds up in front of one gastronomic society or another and people start dancing, their arms held
high, finding their way into the bars, or calling in at one, or several,
of the best-known gastronomic societies.

Tonight, Kika and José Ramon will go to three societies. In Sora-
luce street they stop outside a building with half closed metal
shutters: the *Sociedad Gastronomica Unión Artesana*, or Guild of
Craftsmen. As the door opens and they step into a large room,
with tables arranged along its length so that it looks like a cross
between a restaurant and a bar, they are engulfed by music. A
band is playing the city march, accompanied by members of the
society who, still seated at the dining tables in tall chef's paper-hats,
are wielding drumsticks to beat on flat wooden dishes embellished
with a paper knife and fork. The noise is deafening. Behind the
bar, the waitress is serving endless cups of coffee, glasses of brandy
and liqueurs. A group of members standing there greet Kika and
begin to wax lyrical on the subject of their dinner, a five course
affair. The sauce with the meat was exquisite; according to one,
words could not describe the dish of elvers, according to another,
'the cook bought them alive this morning and what is more, they
were the black-backed sort'.

Soon Kika and José Ramon move on, this time to the most famous
society of all, Gaztelubide. After a pitched battle to get through
the doors they find a table where they can sit down and enjoy
some more of the well-deserved bubbly so typical of the night.
Soon the conversation turns to the societies themselves. Several
young people maintain that they are on the verge of disappearing.
According to one girl, most of the societies are now only patronized
by old men, many of whom seldom do any cooking themselves,
while young couples increasingly have dinner together at home
or in the town's excellent restaurants. Another pessimist argues
that the Basques do not so much love cooking as enjoy eating
well. But others disagree. 'It is the love of good food that always
moves us to cook', said an older member who had overheard the
conversation.

But, as others commented to me the year I saw the *Tamborrada*, the love of good food always moves us to cook. Maybe the societies will need to relax their rules barring women, but I do not think that that is the problem; as long as the love for food survives then the societies will go on flourishing

THE PROFESSIONAL CHEF

If you drive up to Monte Igueldo, one of the twin hills which stand over the bay of San Sebastián like guardians of its security, and then follow the road for a few kilometres, you come to a restaurant in a spectacular setting. On one side, far below, lies a valley broken up into fields and dotted with small homesteads. On the other, is the open expanse of the great Cantabrian sea. This restaurant, Akelarre (also spelt 'Akelaŕe'), is one of the corner-stones of modern Basque cookery and Pedro Subijana, its chef-proprietor, a cheerfully down to earth man instantly recognizable by his huge moustache, is acknowledged throughout Spain as one of the most important figures in the renaissance of Basque cooking through the *nueva cocina vasca*, the new style of cooking.

At Akelarre, which means witches' sabbath, tradition and modernity have gone hand in hand. In the small, but highly organized kitchen, the new and old stand together side by side. Old utensils such as earthenware casseroles, *cazuelas*, are used as often as a whole range of the most up-to-date cooking equipment – double bottomed stainless steel pans, steam and convection ovens, microwaves and contact operated induction ovens. Cast iron frying-pans are used less, but from time to time a miniature version is used to prepare an apple dessert or another speciality of the house. On a long shelf stand dozens of different types of vinegars – Jerez, Modena or locally made cider vinegar – used in the new style of salad dressing and sauces. Nearby, on the floor, are stacked boxes of fresh ingredients, evidence of Pedro's daily morning shopping excursion to the market where he competes against the town's housewives and other chefs for the best of the day: tender baby carrots, *zizak* in a wicker basket, a selection of farmhouse cheeses and large wooden boxes of fish.

Out in the restaurant itself every table has a spectacular view of the sea through large windows. The tables, with immaculate ivory linen tablecloths and fresh flowers, are arranged around the pentagonal shape of the building and on two levels: an outer ring and a raised inner one. In winter, a large fireplace, situated on the raised gallery, becomes the centrepiece. A great stained glass partition in Art Nouveau style separates the dining-room from the lounge where after dinner drinks are served. No detail is spared. A design of an enormous antique fruit dish piled high with dozens of different fruits, a smaller dish containing sweetmeats and next to the dish half a dozen small bottles of vinegar, is printed on the white window blinds, the menu and on the restaurant's writing paper.

Pedro takes all the orders himself, giving his personal attention to every table. If the customer is already a friend, he will recommend the day's speciality; if he is new to the restaurant, Pedro introduces himself first and will try to guide him through the menu. When the customers ask him what he recommends he always talks to them first for a few minutes, so that he can find out what sort of appetite they have, what mood they are in and what the occasion is – repaying somebody, a business engagement or a romantic one. 'There are different dishes for different people and also for one and the same person on different occasions', he explains, smiling broadly behind his moustache. 'You meet lots of people every day and those who are not already friends soon become so. It's such an important part of the job, both to give pleasure and to learn yourself. Your customer or friend will tell you his reaction to a particular dish. Once you have heard several people's views you know straight away whether you are working in the right direction.'

Pedro grew up with the love of good food in his blood. San Sebastián, where he was born and has always lived, is one of the great restaurant cities: a frontier city, influenced gastronomically and in many other ways by France, and the capital of the cider houses and gastronomic societies, where a restaurant must always look to its laurels. Here the housewife is continually trying to present dishes which will pull her husband back to his own table, away from the gastronomic society or evenings out in the bars with his friends. Nearly everyone is an aspiring chef, a chef at heart or an apprentice chef.

Pedro studied at the Catering School in Madrid, under Luis Irizar, one of the fathers of present day cuisine, then worked his way through several restaurants to perfect his skills and after ten years, set up Akelarre. In 1983 he won the National Prize for Gastronomy awarded to the best chef in Spain. Despite success and fame, he is very much a working chef who lives as much in the kitchen as at home. The long working day, which means from nine in the morning through to the early hours of the following day, leaves little time for relaxation. By nine in the morning, he is on the phone placing orders and giving instructions before climbing on to his motorbike to ride into one of the markets, in the centre of town. Here he searches out the best to add to the menu that day, buying in small quantities here and there. Later, somebody will call with the Akelarre van to pick up whatever Pedro has bought: game, good vegetables, beef, excellent fish, delicious fruit from the Navarrese plain, or good farmhouse cheeses from the mountains.

Today he is shopping in San Martín market. He moves from stall to stall, talking as much as buying. Everybody wants to sell him their best produce. He spots some wonderful young garden peas, 'I picked them myself this morning', promises the stallkeeper 'and I am sure that I shall have some more tomorrow, too, if you like them.' He pays and asks her to put them on one side. Then he notices a basket of perfect Russula mushrooms. A special dish for the day begins to take shape in his mind: he can cook the little peas, wild russulas mushrooms and some magnificent lobster that were delivered the evening before. Pedro loves putting dishes together in this way. When the customers come in he tells them about the delicious things that he has found in the market. He tries to pass on his excitement and then they will try the dish.

Pedro's most important purchases are at the fish stalls. The fish are carefully arranged so that the buyer can see their gills clearly; these should be bright red in colour and the eyes, bright and shining. Both these details indicate that the fish is fresh enough for it to be bought. At five in the morning the fishmongers meet for the auction on the quayside at the port of Pasajes and then drive straight to the market, to spend several hours preparing the fish laying it out on the slab. Sometimes the fish is too fresh and it needs to rest for several hours before cooking, otherwise neither the flavour nor the texture are at their very best. The variety is amazing, with all kinds of local rock fish and every size of hake. Pedro looks always for hake caught with a rod and line because this plays a very important role in the final quality of the fish. There is a world of difference between the hake caught by the fishing boats of Fuenterrabía or Bermeo and those which reach the market place via the dragnets of trawlers, where the fish die in the water. Pedro can judge this by the texture of the flesh.

On another stall a small basket of *kokotxas*, or cheeks, occupies a prime central position. This expensive ingredient described by the great Basque writer, José María Busca Isusi as 'the fleshy parts around the gullet of the fish, that is the area between the two bony parts of the lower jaw', began to make its appearance in gastronomic treatises only in the thirties. Since there is only one *kokotxa* per hake, they command very high prices. The traditional way of cooking them is in a green sauce (see page 145), but on occasions Pedro serves them simply coated in egg and flour. The only secret of this recipe lies in the freshness of the *kokotxas* and in frying them in really hot olive oil.

Usually Pedro is back at the restaurant by eleven in the morning with the outline for the dishes of the day shaped in his head. On his return he and his most experienced chef finally organize the new dishes. The menu, which changes seasonally, is a marvellous combination of traditional Basque cooking and the new style influenced by French *nouvelle cuisine*. The traditional dishes, not necessarily the simplest, constitute a third of Akelarre's menu. This type of dish, cooked in Euskadi for a long time, is the food legacy of both the *caserío*, the farmstead, and the *cocina marinera*, the cooking of the fishing villages. There is seafood soup in the style of San Sebastián, a dish which, with small variations, may be found in most of the taverns along the coast; fish cooked on a griddle with garlic and parsley, just as you would find it in the *sidrerías*; plain but creamy *mamia* and *arroz con leche* as good as that from the mountain valley; cheeses from Idiazabal and Roncal to mention but a few. Beans are represented by *alubias rojas de Abendano*, accompanied by spicy *chorizo* sausage, fatty bacon, pig's ear, pork ribs and cabbage. Traditionally these are served with a little dish of chillies in vinegar. The beans, small in size with very dark red skin, a variety grown in this area, are of excellent quality when used in the year they are grown and are called *Abendano* after the name of the *caserío* where one of the waitresses comes from. Her mother sows just one crop and sells them all throughout that year, so the quality is always high. Other dishes, like the *morcilla cocida en berza con salsa de alubias*, black pudding cooked with cabbage with a bean sauce, are Pedro's own creations though based on traditional ingredients, in this case, black pudding, cabbage and beans.

Baked rice with clams in an earthenware dish, arroz con almejas, is one of the most traditional fish and shellfish dishes. It has a sensational flavour and dramatic appearance with the dark clams standing out against the bright white rice.

 To prepare **Arroz con almejas** for two people Pedro takes ¼ kg (8¾ oz) of round grain rice, ¼ kg (8¾ oz) of very fresh clams, 1 clove of garlic, ½ green pepper (finely sliced), olive oil, vegetable stock and salt. He puts on the stove a medium-sized, but quite deep earthenware dish containing some oil and, once it is hot, he adds the green pepper, allowing it to soften a little, then lightly browns the garlic and adds the rice and clams. Finally, he pours over the stock, using three measures of stock to one of rice and cooks it in a moderate oven for about twenty minutes.

Another outstanding dish is hake in a sauce of *kokotxas* and clams, inspired by the popular hake in green sauce. The passion of Basque people for this fish, which is relatively undervalued in most countries, can only be understood when one is able to eat fish of the quality found in the markets of the Basque Country. Pedro also has a theory that the Basques have found a suitable recipe for it where others have not. This is the recipe he is referring to. There are many slight variations; sometimes peas are added or hard-boiled egg, clams or asparagus. This version, however has become particularly renowned.

 To prepare **Merluza en salsa verde** for six people we need 1 kg (2 lbs) of very fresh hake cut into reasonably thick slices, olive oil, 2 cloves of garlic and some finely chopped parsley. Put the oil with the sliced garlic into a traditional earthenware dish. For this sort of recipe it is very important that the oil should not get too hot and that the garlic should stew rather than fry. When the garlic has become slightly golden in colour, add the fish and sprinkle with the parsley. The cooking heat should be low. After a few minutes the hake will begin to release a little whitish liquid, at which stage you should begin to shake the dish gently so that, gradually, the sauce will thicken and the garlic and the oil emulsify after about fifteen minutes.

In summer too, a special *marmitako* fisherman's stew is available, (see p. 46). Pedro's version includes two dried red peppers, uses less tunny and is made with fish stock rather than water.

At Christmas, when snails are traditional, he prepares *caracoles sin trabajo con salsa de berros*, effortless snails with watercress sauce.

Effortless to eat rather than to cook, unfortunately, but delicious nonetheless. When using fresh snails, the first thing that you have to do is cure them, that is to say, wash them in plenty of water containing salt and vinegar in order to rid them of all the slime. This process will need repeating several times. Then put them into a pan of cold water and leave to cook for about one hour. Once they are done remove them from their shells and take off the soft portion which has a bitter flavour. If they still seem tough boil a little longer. This recipe should always be made with fresh snails.

 Pedro allows 10 snails per person for **Caracoles sin trabajo con salsa de berros**. Put a knob of butter and a few drops of oil in a saucepan. In this sauté 2 cloves of garlic. Add the snails and flambé with a little brandy and a similar quantity of sherry. Remove the thickest stalks from a small bunch of watercress and chop them finely. Add the cress to the pan, followed by 4 tablespoons of tomato sauce (see p. 113) and 2 of *salsa espanola* made with a brown roux, brown stock, diced belly of pork, vegetables, herbs, tomato purée and wine. Roll out two thin rounds of puff pastry, brush with beaten egg and place a whole snail shell in the centre of each. Place them in a moderate oven for about ten minutes and once they are ready cut them through horizontally and spread the snails and their sauce on the lower half. Replace the other piece of pastry with the shell on it to make a lid.

The other strand of the menu at Akelarre has developed from the New Basque cooking – *Euskal Sukaldaritza Berria* – which began to take shape in the late seventies. Its fundamental precepts, raw materials of superlative quality and the strictly seasonal use of ingredients, as well as many of its techniques, such as shorter cooking times and reduced use of animal fats, are drawn directly from its older French cousin. Subijana and Juan Mari Arzak, the most flamboyant of the Basque chefs, found their new direction after hearing Paul Bocuse speak at the 1976 Gastronomic Round Table in Madrid. 'Suddenly it became obvious,' remembers Pedro 'that Basque cooking possessed all the inherent elements to raise it to its proper place as one of the most interesting and original cuisines of the world. We realized that everything they were preaching regarding their cuisine was true of Basque cooking. It had been at the back of our minds for a long time, but without us really appreciating it.' But the *nueva cocina vasca* is by no means simply an imitation of *nouvelle cuisine*. Pedro finds that the French version is much more homogenous than the Spanish, a reflection of the centralization of culture which makes itself felt as early as infant school. In Spain, where each autonomous region has kept its particularities, *nueva cocina* has been interpreted in very different ways. Certainly the dishes that the Basque chefs have created are, almost without exception, of Basque inspiration, their ingredients following the distinctive culinary tradition. This is hardly surprising. There are few places where chefs would think about cooking in quite the same terms of idealistic pride and 'integrity' as in the Basque Country. They firmly believe that cooking is part of the heritage of a nation or region and that the ritual of eating and drinking well are an essential part of Basque idiosyncrasy. They can be identified by the way they eat and cook. 'It is only logical that we should defend the national identity, of which we are so proud, through some part of our culture', says Pedro. 'Over the centuries we have defended our identity against every attempt to absorb it which we have been subjected to. In any case, breaking with tradition does not mean losing your own culture. Each one of the dishes which have been added to the culinary repertoire and which today we think of as classic, was once new and a break with tradition. A good example of this is the *baba-txikis* soup (broadbean), which after the discovery of America became red-bean soups or various potato stews.'

Tradition has not always been so carefully nurtured, at least not in San Sebastián, where over a century after the French Revolution international cuisine reigned supreme to the detriment of the more original, indigenous cooking. During the whole of the period, but particularly in the *Belle Epoque*, San Sebastián was the traditional summer holiday resort of the aristocracy. Their cooks and chefs, while spending the summer months cooking for their masters, would pass on their experience and techniques to the local people hired to help in the kitchen during the family's stay in the north. Today, happily, the situation is reversed. The figure of the Basque chef has crossed both national and international frontiers and the specialities and characteristics of Basque cookery can be found in London, Paris and New York. In Spain itself it is unusual for a place with any pretensions to gastronomic excellence not to have one or more Basque dishes on its menu, presided over by a Basque chef, and the best restaurants in Madrid and many other provincial capitals, are Basque. Zalacain, considered to be Spain's most prestigious restaurant, has a Navarrese chef, Benjamin Urdiain.

The new recipes of the *nueva cocina vasca*, reflect this sense of regional identity. They have been evolved by chefs handling produce from the daily market, experimenting among friends while continuing to respect the preferences of their compatriots. It is striking, for example, that fish dishes still make up over three-quarters of any menu and have been the most successful of the new dishes. Here are three fine dishes which make the point. The first is Juan Mari Arzak's recipe for a fish terrine made with *cabracho*, scorpion fish, called *krabarroka* in Basque. It was one of the great early successes of the *nueva cocina*.

 For a **Pastel de krabarroka** to feed six we need 500 g (1 lb) of scorpion fish, cleaned and with the head and scales removed, 250 g (8 oz) fresh tomato sauce, 250 ml (8 oz) of single cream, 8 eggs, 1 leek, 1 carrot, a little butter, breadcrumbs, salt and white pepper. Peel the carrot and clean the leek and put them with the fish in a pan of water to simmer. When it is cooked remove the fish from the bones, flake it and set aside. Grease a mould with butter and sprinkle with breadcrumbs. In a basin beat the eggs, add the cream, the fish, salt and pepper and mix well. Pour the mixture into the mould and cook in a *bain-marie* in a moderate oven for just one hour. This recipe is served cold with a mayonnaise made with peanut oil and a dash of sherry vinegar.

In the early days of *Euskal Sukaldaritza Berria*, since it was a complete break with tradition, Basque chefs began to add cream to some dishes which caused considerable comment. In some cases, certainly, it was used excessively, but in others it produced new classics. One of Pedro Subijana's recipes, probably his best known, sea bass with green peppercorns, illustrates this perfectly.

For **Lubina a la pimienta verde** we need for four people 4 boned sea bass steaks weighing 200g (7oz) each, 1 chopped shallot, 75g (2oz) green peppercorns, 15g (½oz) butter, 100ml (3½floz) of olive oil, 100ml (3½floz) of apple brandy, 200ml (7floz) of single cream. Place butter, oil and chopped shallot in a skillet and add the sea bass with the skin side up. Incorporate the peppercorns and flambé with the apple brandy. Pour over the cream and put in the oven for seven minutes. Take out the fish and reduce the sauce. Check the seasoning and pour the sauce over the fish when ready to serve.

As a final example of traditional cooking set in a more up-to-date context, here is Benjamín Urdiaín's recipe for sea bream with a white wine sauce. He uses a white wine with great character from Rueda, in the Duero region, so the dish reflects its character.

To prepare **Besugo al vino blanco** for six people we need 3 sea bream of approx 1kg (2lb) each, 50g (1¾oz) of garlic, 50ml (1¾floz) of Rueda wine, 50ml (1¾floz) of sea bream stock, 300ml (10½floz) of pure olive oil, 250ml (8¾floz) of fresh cream, salt and white pepper. Clean the fish and remove the head and bones. Split each fish in half. Make 300ml (½ a pint) of stock with the head and bones. Slightly cook the garlic cloves (unpeeled) in 50ml (1¾floz) of olive oil. Add the white wine and the fish stock and reduce by one half. Add the cream and boil for seven minutes. Put through a blender and then pass through a very fine strainer. Adjust the seasoning and set aside. Season the pieces of bream, place on a tray with 250ml (8¾floz) of olive oil and bake in the oven for approximately twelve minutes. Put the bream on a serving dish and cover them with the creamy garlic and wine sauce. Serve with green vegetables.

When the Basque chefs launched *nueva cocina vasca*, they also aimed to rescue traditional recipes passed on by word of mouth; they are followed accurately, with no frills. In this respect, there are far more Spanish than French Basque recipes passed down without any written versions since the southern part of Euskadi, on the Spanish side of the frontier, has always enjoyed a more lively and very distinct gastronomic tradition.

 Eltzekaria, a traditional soup from the province of Laburdi, or Labourdie, and popular on both sides of the Pyrenees, is one such recipe that the chefs have revived. For six people you need ¼ kg (8 oz) white beans, soaked overnight, a medium-sized cabbage – finely chopped, 150 g (5 oz) of finely chopped onion, 2 cloves of garlic-crushed, 80 g (3 oz) of lard, salt, pepper and 1½ litres (3 pints) of water. Melt the lard in an earthenware pot and sauté the onion until it begins to brown, then add the water, beans, cabbage and garlic. Cook slowly for two to three hours or until the beans are soft. Sometimes a few drops of cider vinegar are added before serving.

Often, in *nueva cocina*, traditional recipes are interpreted rather than faithfully reproduced. It is not necessarily a question of a new version substituting the traditional one in every restaurant, but rather that different versions contribute to a more comprehensive, contemporary Basque cuisine. For example, eggs scrambled with wild mushrooms and fresh garlic might inspire a *hojaldre* or *millefeuilles* of eggs scrambled with *perretxikos* mushrooms or traditional boiled cabbage may be stuffed with duck and served with a celery purée. Equally in Pedro's kitchen a lettuce and tomato salad with a little canned tuna fish and olives becomes a salad of tomatoes from Igueldo with marinated fresh tunny fish, and twin pepper and tomato sauces. This, to my mind, is one of Pedro's supreme recipes. It has the power to make you feel, immediately, that you are in the Basque Country.

 For **Ensalada de tomate del país y bonito marinado** you need for 4 people 400 g (14 oz) of gutted tunny on the bone, 1 lemon, virgin olive oil, cider vinegar, 4 small tomatoes each weighing 80 to 100 g (3 to 3⅓ oz) and not too ripe, 2 very red, ripe tomatoes for the sauce and for the salad, 3 green peppers, several basil leaves and a handful of chervil leaves. First make sure the tunny is thoroughly cleaned and remove any dark patches. Cut the fish lengthwise into slices about 10 cm long and then cut very thin fillets, also 10 cm long, off these lengthwise, making them as wide as possible (usually 4–5 cm). Season with salt and pepper and put them to marinate with a little lemon rind and a few drops each of cider vinegar and olive oil. Leave in the fridge to marinate for at least five hours. Meanwhile chop the ripe tomatoes, season with salt and pepper and a few drops of lemon juice, strain and refrigerate. Do the same thing with the green peppers – though it may be necessary to add a little water to thin the consistency and then they need cooking a little since this improves its flavour. On each plate arrange a few very thin slices of tomato which have already been dressed with salt, oil and vinegar, but have been drained well. Gently pour over the tomato sauce and then the green pepper sauce, running the colour into each other. Arrange the slices of marinated tunny on top. Decorate with little basil leaves around the edges and some sprigs of chervil on top.

In the majority of duck recipes cooked in the traditional Basque style, the duck is browned and later transferred to an earthenware pot to cook for a long time with wine and other ingredients such as onions, carrots, etc., always on the top of the stove. Pedro uses first class ducks which are tender and need very little time in the oven, and contrary to the old style of cooking in which the meat was dried and needed to be flavoured by the rest of the ingredients, Pedro's ducks retained their own taste and the other ingredients, which in any case are also very different to ones used before, such as wine vinegar, green peppercorns, etc. just add complexity to the final result. He buys his ducks from a nearby farm where they feed them as though for their own table and this is an excellent guarantee.

 To prepare a **Pato de caserío medio asado a la salsa de Cava**, underdone roast farmhouse duckling in a sauce made with Cava sparkling wine, you will need 2 ducks, each weighing about 1 kg (2 lbs), 1 medium-sized onion, ½ a bulb of garlic, cut cross-wise, 100 ml (3.5 fl oz) of olive oil, 500 ml (17 fl oz) of Cava sparkling wine, 25 g (¾ oz) of sugar, a few drops of wine vinegar, a twist of orange rind and of lemon, a few green peppercorns, 100 ml (3.5 fl oz) of duck essence (juices previously reduced), 1 small glass of Cava wine. Dress and clean the ducks thoroughly, season them inside and out with salt and pepper and coat them well in olive oil. Place them on a suitable-sized baking tray and spread over the bottom of this the onion, cut into rings, and the ½ bulb of garlic. When the oven is really hot put in the ducks. It is important to keep an eye on the roasting process, basting the birds constantly with the fat which collects in the tin. They should be golden brown on the outside but almost raw in the middle. Cook for about fifteen minutes. Pour off the excess oil, pour in the Cava wine and transfer the duck to a plate or board. Cut off the breast and leg portion, cut the carcases into pieces and return to the roasting tin. Set aside the ducks' joints on a serving dish. Add to the roasting tin the duck essence and green peppercorns and return to the hot oven. In a small saucepan heat the sugar, a few drops of vinegar and the orange and lemon rind until it begins to caramelize. Add the Cava wine and bring the mixture back to the boil, then strain the mixture from the roasting tin into the pan. The sauce is ready, taste and adjust the seasoning. Put the duck joints, skin uppermost, under a hot grill to crispen the skin; then add the sauce and serve. Pedro Subijana recommends puréed watercress as an accompaniment to this dish.

In the same way, Pedro has reworked ideas from traditional Basque *pastelería* into new ideas, like this *millefeuille* of figs with walnut sauce. His father was an exceptional pastry maker and he has inherited a love for this difficult speciality.

 To prepare a **Hojaldre de higos frescos con salsa de nueces** you need for four people 4 sheets of flaky pastry, measuring 12 × 5 cm, flaked almonds, icing sugar, 8 fresh figs, peeled and cut into slices, ¼ litre (8 fl oz) of confectioner's custard, a few drops of rum. For the walnut sauce ½ litre (17 fl oz) of milk, a little lemon rind, ¼ of a stick of cinnamon, 100 g (3 ½ oz) of sugar, 150 g (5 ½ oz) of shelled walnuts, a little cream and breadcrumbs. First, using a marble slab, Pedro makes the pastry. He prepares a mound of 500 g (1 lb) of flour, to which he adds 10 g of salt, a few drops of lemon juice, 284 ml (½ pint) of cold water and 100 g (3 ½ oz) of the 500 g (1 lb) of butter he will need for the whole preparation, slightly softened. He incorporates the butter into the flour and mixes the ingredients to form a dough, without handling it more than necessary, and using just one hand to form a rough ball. With a knife he makes two cuts to form a cross on top of this and then sets the dough aside to rest for a while. He sets to work again rolling out the dough with a floured rolling pin in four directions to immitate the shape of a green cross, leaving the pastry thicker in the centre. He takes the remainder of the butter and squashes it slightly with the palm of his hand in the middle of the sheet of pastry. He folds the arms of the cross inwards to cover the butter. Then he rolls the pastry out once more, using deft, even movements to form a rectangular shape. He folds this into three and then repeats the rolling process, after which he again leaves the pastry to rest for about twenty minutes covered with a cloth. He carries out the rolling and folding procedure until the pastry has been rolled out and folded six times in all. To prepare the rest of the recipe, put the milk to heat with the cinnamon and lemon rind and meanwhile crush the walnuts with a pestle and mortar and mix in the sugar. When the milk comes to the boil, add the walnuts and simmer gently for half an hour. Lastly sprinkle in a few fine breadcrumbs and add a drop of cream. Leave this to cool when it should form a thick custard. Sprinkle the sheets of pastry with flaked almonds and place them in a moderate oven to cook. Just before taking the pastry out of the oven dust it with the icing sugar which will allow it to caramelize a little. Once the pastry is cooked remove it from the oven and set it aside to cool. Split each pastry in half, horizontally, and put a couple of teaspoons of the confectioner's custard inside, flavoured with rum (old rum, if possible). On top of the custard arrange the slices of fig or any fresh fruit such as apricots and then replace the top piece of pastry and dust again with icing sugar. Make a pool of the walnut sauce on the base of the serving dish and set the *milhojas* on this. It can be decorated with fresh fruit sauce around the edge.

During the day Pedro rarely gets the chance to take a break. In the morning there are countless small but important things to do: he organizes the selection of desserts to be made, works with the *souschef* on any new dishes and keeps an eye on all the basic preparations. At half past twelve, everyone breaks for the staff lunch and, if he has the time, Pedro sits down briefly at the table. Half an hour later, Akelarre opens its doors and customers begin to arrive. It is a time of tension and haste: of vigilance to be sure that each dish is perfect. All the members of staff have to make use of every bit of their expertise. It is a team effort. Pedro, checking everything, has to be in the kitchen, in the dining-room, everywhere at once. Even when the rush is over he is busy, moving from table to table, asking customers if they have enjoyed their meal, gauging their reactions to new dishes, greeting regulars and friends. Sometimes he has to sit down and have coffee with some of them as they have come to talk to him. Finally, later in the afternoon, he goes home for a few brief hours of family life. They all have supper together, sometimes he has a rest, or sometimes he goes for a walk with the three children. By half past eight, though, he must be back in the restaurant again and ready for the evening session. Towards the end of the session, at about eleven o'clock, they check the stores and make up the orders, noting the most urgent telephone calls which will have to be made first thing the following morning. Once again he is lost amongst the tables talking now with a friend, now with a customer. At last the day draws to a close. There may be a moment to have a drink with a friend who calls in the evening. Brandy is one of Pedro's idiosyn-cratic whims and in his office on a large shelf, he keeps fifteen different Armagnacs.

Sunday, his day of rest, is dedicated to his children. But this does not mean that he escapes the kitchen. He cooks their favourite dishes, for example grilled fish with garlic and cider vinegar or meat casseroles. He often asks his children to help him clean squid or prepare vegetables so that, almost in play, they get used to handling all sorts of ingredients and learn different ways of prepar-ing them. 'Even if you are not going to be a chef, it is a good thing to feel at home at the stove', he says 'because it brings enjoy-ment and it means that you are not dependent on somebody who probably does not cook things in the way that you like'.

During these relaxed Sunday cooking sessions, Pedro has formu-lated many of his best dishes. One, for example, a salad of pasta with elvers, he stumbled upon while he was trying to find an alternative to frying them. Substituting fresh oil for cooked makes the dish more digestible.

To make **Ensalada de angulas con pasta** he uses 200 g (7 oz) of elvers, 2 tablespoons of olive oil, the juice of ¼ lemon and 1 clove of garlic for the elvers. For the pasta he allows 100 g (3½ oz) of fresh egg pasta, 100 g (3⅓ oz) of fresh spinach pasta, 20 g (½ oz) of butter, 2 lettuce leaves, fresh ground black pepper, a few drops of lemon juice and salt and for the salad 200 g (7 oz) of chicory, chopped, 2–3 endive leaves, a few radishes, olive oil, cider vinegar and salt. Peel and cut in half a garlic clove and rub the bottom of an earthenware pot with it. Tip in the elvers. Add the olive oil and lemon juice. Mix well. Before serving remove any excess dressing. Chop the lettuce, endive and chicory. Add the radishes and the carrot, season with salt. Pour over a little olive oil and the cider vin-egar. Before serving, as before, remove any excess dressing. Bring plenty of water to the boil in a large saucepan, add salt and the pasta. When the pasta is ready drain off the water. Place a little butter in a frying pan, add the pasta and sauté for one minute. At this point add fresh ground black pepper and a drop of fresh lemon juice to the pasta. Each plate should be served with the elvers in the centre, then a ring of the salad, finishing with the slightly warm pasta (the pasta should be cooked once the elvers and salad have been arranged on each plate). Although cider vinegar is recommended by chef Subijana for this delicate preparation a few drops of sherry vinegar are also delicious.

Other simple dishes he makes are more traditional. One in particular, the recipe for *guibelurdiñas* or russulas is a popular one which you can taste in *asadores*, or barbecues and bars. It can be used for all kinds of fungi.

 To prepare **Russulas** for four people you need 1.5kg (3lbs) of mushrooms, 200ml (7floz) of olive oil, 2 cloves of garlic, chopped parsley and salt. For russulas, Pedro removes the stalks, which he slices and soaks in salted water for a while, leaving the caps whole. Then he dampens the hotplate with salted water and begins to put the caps on it with the slices on top. The heat must be quite high and as they cook quickly he sprinkles them with a little salted water so that they do not lose their moisture. They only need cooking for two or three minutes on each side. Meanwhile he fries the garlic in oil until golden brown and adds a little chopped parsley. He arranges the mushrooms on individual heated plates with some of the slices on top and pours over a little oil with the garlic and parsley.

Pedro's most cherished success is neither the recognition by other Spanish, and French chefs, nor by the media, but that of a public which is closer to his heart, the people of San Sebastián who pack out the restaurant every Sunday for large family lunches. The recurrance of this, week after week, still gives Pedro a real thrill, for he knows that these are the most ruthless critics of all. For them, he knows he must provide a perfect blend of the old and the new and no less.

'The love of good food is imbibed with a mother's milk', says Pedro. 'You are born into a family where good food is considered important, where, from your tenderest years, you learn to be more demanding. Everything happens around the dinner table. This is not so much a cliché as a custom, and not a difficult one to understand since human beings spend so much of their lives eating. If they eat well and with enjoyment so much the better for them.'

GLOSSARY

ALBACORA Albacore, *Thunnus alalunga*. Small tuna common in the Bay of Biscay; the meat is less heavy than that of the *atun. See also* FISH.

ALUBIAS Haricot beans. Usually bought dried.

AMACHU Mother.

ANCHOA Anchovy, *Engraulis encrasicolus. See also* FISH.

ANGULA Elver, or baby eel.

ARROZ Rice; a dish made with rice.

ASADOR Barbecue; barbecue restaurant.

ATUN Bluefin tuna, *Thunnus thynnus*. Largest of the tuna family, popular in Basque cookery particularly with tomato sauces or grilled. *See also* FISH.

BACALAO Salt-cod. *See also* FISH.

BESUGO Red sea bream, *Pagellus bogaraveo* or *P. centrodontus*. The best of the sea breams. *See also* FISH.

BONITO Bonito, *Sarda sarda*. Small tuna produced in the same ways as *atun*. The flesh is lighter in colour. *See also* FISH.

CABRACHO Scorpion fish, *Scorpaena scrofa. See also* FISH.

CASERIO A farm house; *caserío-txakolí* is a winery and inn where *txakolí* wine is made and sold.

CAVA WINE Spanish sparkling wine prepared by the *méthode champenoise*.

CAZUELA Earthenware casserole; a dish prepared in this.

CEBOLLA Onion.

CHIQUITO Small glass of wine.

CHORICERO PEPPER A variety of green or red pepper. The term is commonly used for dried sweet red pepper.

CHORIZO Sausage flavoured with pepper, *pimentón* and garlic.

COSTERA Fishing season.

CUADRILLAS A group of men.

DORADA Gilthead bream, *Sparus auratus. See also* FISH.

ENSALADA Salad.

EUSKADI The Basque country; *euskal sukaldaritza berria* is the new Basque cuisine.

FISH In most of the fish recipes, one kind may be substituted for another of the same general type – white or oily. Far more important is that the fish should be very fresh. In the tunny recipes any type of fresh tunny (but not canned) may be used. However, scorpion fish, with its unusual flavour, must be used for the *pastel de krabarroka*. This fish is the famous *rascasse* said to be indispensable for making *bouillabaisse*, and is sometimes imported for that purpose by very serious fish shops. Monkfish is also irreplaceable, but easy enough to find.

FUERO Local law conferring privilege on an organization.

GUIBELURDINA Wild mushroom, *Russula cynaxanta. See also* MUSH-ROOMS.

HOJALDRE *Millefeuille*, dish made with puff pastry.

HORNO Oven.

HUEVO Egg.

KAIKU One-piece birchwood milking pail.

KOTOTXA Cheek pieces of hake; a delicacy.

KUPELA, KUPELAK Wine or cider vat.

LECHE Milk.

LUBINA Sea bass, *Dicentrarchus labrax. See also* FISH.

MARINERA, A LA In the style of fisherfolk.

MERLUZA Hake, *Merluccius merluccius. See also* FISH.

MORCILLA black pudding.

MUSHROOMS Many of the species mentioned on pages 6–10 also grow wild in Britain and temperate North America. Most species grow in autumn, apart from morels (spring) and St George's mushroom (early summer). Common mushrooms identical or closely related to those in this book are as follows: *zizak*, St George's mushroom (*Tricholoma gambosum*, not *T. georgii* as you would suppose, has that name in Britain), or use other *Tricholoma* species such as the blewit (*T. saevum*) and wood blewit (*T. nudum*); related to *guibelurdiña* are several *Russula* species, of which the green capped *R. virescens* is probably the best; similar to *Boletus aereus* is the cep (*B. edulis*) and several other types of *Boletus* are common; *ziza-ori*, chanterelle (*Cantharellus edulis*); *karraspina*, morel (*Morchella esculenta*, *M. vulgaris* is similar); *galanperna*, parasol (*Lepiota procera*); *esnegorri*, milk cap (*Lactarius deliciosus*); ink cap or shaggy mane (*Coprinus comatus*); *berrengorri*, field mushroom (*Agaricus campestris*) and several other *Agaricus* species (the cultivated mushroom, *A. bisporus*, is an uninteresting relative). Do not look for the rare *kuletos*, Caesar's agaric (*Amanita caesarea*): if you think you have found one, it will almost certainly turn out to be a pale specimen of the poisonous fly agaric (*A. muscaria*) with its distinctive white flecks washed off the cap by rain. You can buy some wild mushrooms in good delicatessens: field mushrooms; occasionally chanterelles, fresh or dried; morels, dried or in cans; and ceps, almost always dried but quite easy to find, usually under their Italian name *funghi porcini* or German *Steinpilze*. One kind of wild mushroom can be substituted for another, except for *Tricholoma* species, most of which have a mild flavour. A reasonable way to fake a mixture of wild mushrooms is to use cultivated mushrooms and add a few dried ceps or Chinese dried mushrooms (these are shiitake, *Lentinus edodes*, and are widely available from oriental delicatessens: they are dried whole and have distinctive dark caps with white cracks). Soak the dried mushrooms until soft (ceps need several hours, shiitake 20 minutes), strain the soaking water and add it to the recipe. Dried mushrooms are too strong flavoured really to use on their own in a recipe containing a large quantity of mushrooms.

NUEVA COCINA VASCA New style of Basque cookery.

OLIVE OIL The most popular oil in Spain. It is extracted in several stages. The oil from the first pressing, called 'extra virgin', has a fine olive flavour. Virgin oil that does not meet the highest grading standard is refined and then blended with premier quality oil to create olive oil.

OLLA, OLLO Cooking pot; dish prepared in a pot.

PASTEL A cake pie, or even pâté; *pastelito* is a little one; *pastelería* means pâtisserie.

PELOTA Basque national ball game.

PESCADO General term for fish.

PIL-PIL, AL Method of cooking fish with oil and garlic.

PIMENTON Sweet or hot red pepper condiment. Quite easy to obtain, but at a pinch paprika can be used instead.

PIMIENTO Sweet pepper.

PIPERADE Cooked dish of tomatoes and peppers lightened with eggs.

PROBATEKO Tasting of wine or cider.

QUESO Cheese.

RAPE Monkfish, *Lophius piscatorius*. *See also* FISH.

REVUELTO Literally 'turned over'; a dish of scrambled eggs.

SALSA Sauce.

SIDRERIA Cider house, often one open to the public for tasting and food.

SOPA Soup; sop (bread used to take up liquid).

TALO Maize cake.

TAPA Any of an amazing variety of snacks eaten with wine.

TORTILLA Flat omelette.

TXAKOLI A young, sharp, slightly sparkling rosé or white wine; not unlike Portuguese *vinho verde*, which may be used as a substitute in recipes.

TXISTORRA Sausage with spices and garlic.

TXISTU Basque wind instrument, played by a *txistulary*.

VIZCAINA, A LA In the style of Biscay province.

ZIZAK Wild mushroom of the genus *Tricholoma*. *See also* MUSHROOMS.

GENERAL INDEX

INDEX OF RECIPES